G000126575

BRITAIN IN OLD PHOTOGRAPHS

AROUND PLYMOUTH

T O M B O W D E N

ALAN SUTTON PUBLISHING LIMITED

Alan Sutton Publishing Limited
Phoenix Mill · Far Thrupp · Stroud
Gloucestershire · GL5 2BU

First published 1995

British Library Cataloguing in Publication Data.
A catalogue record for this book is available from
the British Library.

ISBN 0-7509-0905-6

Copyright © Tom Bowden, 1995

Cover photographs: (front) Harriet Butler in
the doorway of her shop, Stoke, *c.* 1905; (back)
Strolling on the Hoe, 1912.

Typeset in 9/10 Sabon.
Typesetting and origination by
Alan Sutton Publishing Limited.
Printed in Great Britain by
Ebenezer Baylis, Worcester.

To my children Anne and Martin

The Hoe and Sound, *1910.*

Contents

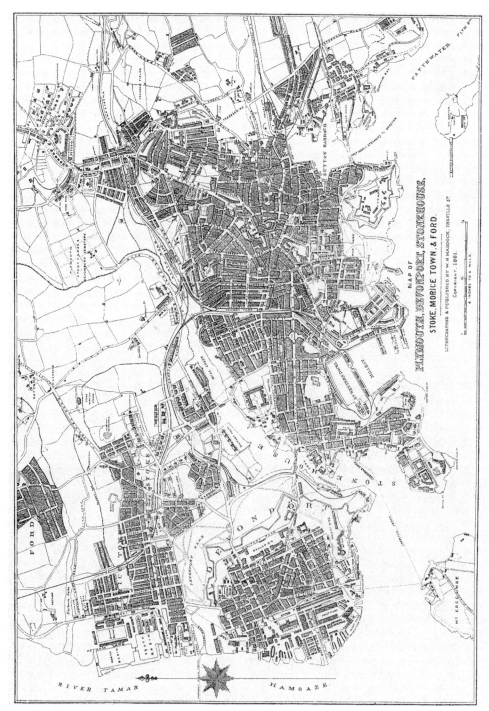

Plymouth, Devonport and Stonehouse, 1881.

Introduction

We have been collecting picture postcards of Plymouth for many years and it seemed a good idea to show them to other people. To be honest my wife, Pam, started the collection and I jumped on the bandwagon. I was born in Torpoint and Pam was born in Stonehouse. We married in St Mark's Church, Ford and lived in Plymouth while I worked in Devonport Dockyard. Then the Royal Navy frogmarched us off to Bath and elsewhere around the United Kingdom. So, we look back and appreciate Plymouth, its history, and its setting, where others may take everything for granted. I have decided upon the format for the book, selected the photographs, written the captions, produced some maps, and now need to explain a few things in this introduction.

I am an engineer and not a historian or journalist, although, over the years, I have read and admired people like Crispin Gill, J.C. Trewin, R.A.J. Walling, A.L. Clamp, and Chris Robinson. I have a different viewpoint and am not only interested in history and factual reporting, within the scope of this book, but in how the photographer works; the detail in the picture and the people in the street. I also try to supply facts in my captions and little opinion. Who is interested in my views anyway? My overall aim is to provide a galaxy of photographs of old Plymouth, with interesting maps and worthwhile captions, to give hours of enjoyment. The book covers the period from the 1890s to the 1970s, from a Victorian and Edwardian age, to the birth of the city, then tumult and destruction in the Blitz, and its rebirth to become the fine modern city it is today. I hope that this volume will provide readers with a vivid impression of the old city, evoke nostalgic memories for many, and give pleasure to residents and visitors alike.

The reader will see that I move across the city from west to east. The central part of the book is the guided tour around the winding streets of the old city before the war, followed by the rebuilding of Plymouth after the Blitz in 1941. There is also a section on schooldays and sporting times, and in the last section we look at some interesting places outside the old city boundary. The three maps supplied should enable everyone to locate the places mentioned in the text.

In selecting the photographs I realize that it is inevitable that you will have seen some before and that some will be new to you. Also, in writing the captions I have tried to cater for those who know little of Plymouth. I must apologize, therefore, for sometimes stating the obvious. My most fondly imagined reader is a lady, with her grandchildren around her, explaining how grandad and grandma used to meet at Derry's Clock and go courting on the Hoe.

There is a thread of personal experience here and there, but I hope I haven't been too self indulgent. I expect I have 'come unstuck' somewhere in the mass of detail: I'm not perfect of course. Sometimes a picture inspires some thoughts and emotions, which I try to express in words. There is joy, sadness, humour and fantasy here, and I hope you can find it. Finally, I must thank my dear wife for her help and forbearance. I hope you all enjoy this little book, especially those who can remember the old times.

Tom Bowden
1995

Fore Street, Devonport, 1908.

Section One

DEVONPORT

No. 9 tram in Fore Street, Devonport, ready to turn into Chapel Street, c. 1900.

Fore Street, Devonport, looking east from the Royal Sailors Rest, *c.* 1910. A familiar and nostalgic view of old Devonport with a mass of large and small businesses and places of entertainment. On the left is the Royal Hotel, with British Home Stores, Tozer's, Lipton's, Burton's, Marks & Spencer's, the Military Hotel and the Electric Theatre on the skyline. To the right is Woolworths, the Prince George Hotel, Underwood's, the Co-operative Society, Devonport post office, and the Tivoli Theatre. I remember going to the 'pictures' in Fore Street as a boy of ten in 1939. If it was an adult category film at the Electric, the Forum, or the Tivoli you had to ask someone to take you in. The entry fee was four old pence, or threepence for up in the 'gods', and I watched films about the Dead-end Kids, or Hopalong Cassidy, or Captain Marvel as I munched my way through a pen'orth of sweets from Woolworths.

Fore Street, Devonport, near the Electric Cinema, looking west, *c*. 1939. On the left is Devonport post office, which was on the corner of Chapel Street and Fore Street. It was built in 1849 and had an elegant semicircular portico like the famed Temple of Tivoli. The nearby Tivoli Theatre took its name from this building. The Forum Cinema, on the right, was built just before the war and survived the coming inferno. It is interesting to note that many of the buildings in Devonport and Plymouth which did survive were new buildings using modern construction methods.

Fore Street, Devonport, after the Blitz, April 1941. A similar view to the one opposite, but now showing the massive destruction of Fore Street. The vast majority of buildings, including the Tivoli Theatre, Devonport post office, the Electric Theatre, the Hippodrome, Alhambra Theatre, and many other well-known businesses, were reduced to rubble or a gutted shell.

Dockyard gate, west end of Fore Street, *c.* 1905. Beyond the gateway can be seen the dockyard church tower on the right and, on the left, a tall column with a belltower. This bell was rung at the start and finish of work. It came from the French ship *Tonnant* captured by Nelson at the Battle of the Nile. On the left side of this photograph is the façade of the Royal Sailors' Rest.

The Royal Sailors' Rest, Fore Street, 1913. Affectionately known as 'Aggie Weston's', and built by Dames Agnes Weston and Sophia Wintz, it opened on 8 May 1876 to provide good meals and accommodation for sailors. Later a large hall, known as Queen Victoria Hall, was added: it opened on 17 January 1905 and provided a very popular restaurant and sleeping accommodation for 800. Dames Agnes Weston and Sophia Wintz were God-fearing and teetotal ladies who were concerned for the welfare of young sailor boys. In 1873 there were nearly 4,000 boys being trained for the Royal Navy in training ships like HMS *Impregnable*, HMS *Implacable* and HMS *Lion*. In more than forty-five years of speaking, corresponding, and fund-raising, these ladies became vitally involved in all aspects affecting the well-being of sailors and their wives and families.

The Royal Sailors' Rest, destroyed 22 April 1941. Both the Portsmouth and Devonport 'Aggie Weston's' were destroyed during the war. The trustees of the organization opened a new Portsmouth Rest in 1952. The new Devonport Royal Sailor's Rest, outside the dockyard gate in Albert Road, was opened in 1959.

Royal Albert Hospital, New Passage Hill, Devonport, *c.* 1905. The hospital opened on 1 December 1863 and was enlarged to 162 beds in 1867, and grew further in later years. It was supported entirely by voluntary contributions and many civilians and servicemen helped in management and fund-raising activities. In 1948 it became part of the National Health Service and changed its name to the South Devon & East Cornwall Hospital, Devonport. In 1963, its centenary year, the hospital changed its title again to Devonport Section of the Plymouth General Hospital, although local people always regarded it as the 'Royal Albert'. The NHS then decided to close the hospital and it was demolished in 1983. The land was then sold off for housing development.

Raglan Barracks, Devonport, 1907. The troops are on parade in front of their accommodation blocks. The barracks extended from Fore Street to Cumberland Road and the main archway (with royal coat of arms) was built in 1853–6 by Captain Fowke. The Electric Theatre and the spire of St Paul's Church, Devonport, can be seen in the distance.

Devonport Technical College, 1914. The words 'Devonport Municipal Science Art & Technical School' were emblazoned along the front of the building when it was built in the 1890s. This bold Victorian building, on its triangular site in Paradise Road, is for me a nostalgic reminder of the 1940s and studying in those bare classrooms and laboratories, then meeting my girlfriend and walking her home, across Devonport Park.

Funeral procession for submariners, King's Road railway station, Devonport, 1905. The Royal Navy had thirteen small A class submarines built in 1904–5. Submarine A8 was launched in January 1905, but foundered on 8 June off Plymouth Breakwater; fifteen men were lost. The procession passes with sailors carrying wreaths and the coffins borne on gun carriages. In the background can be seen the Brickfields recreation ground, Devonport Column, and a number of church spires.

The Old Chapel, junction of Duke and George Streets, Devonport, c. 1910. The chapel was built for the Unitarians as a place of worship in 1790. The congregation diminished over the years, and in 1801 the chapel was converted to a public house. Today the building is still there but is no longer trading.

The Old Chapel interior, c. 1910. The bar is a horseshoe shape with two old tills, and barrels of beer and port stand ready. There is also an old stove, tables and chairs, water jugs and jugs on the wall; a gallery is at the back with adverts for Guinness, Bass, Worthington, and Burton ales. The pub is closed, or is it full of ghostly drinkers?

Devonport Town Hall, Devonport Column and the Egyptian Library, 1906. By 1818 John Foulston, an architect from London, had designed a group of classic buildings in Plymouth including the Royal Theatre, Royal Hotel and the Athenaeum. In 1821 he also designed the grand Devonport Town Hall with Doric pillars, at the top of Ker Street, and the building was much admired. King George IV approved proposals for Plymouth Dock to become Devonport on 1 January 1824. There was great rejoicing, and Foulston was again approached and asked to design this 125 ft triumphal column to celebrate the event. Foulston also experimented with the Egyptian Library, seen on the right, which later became the Oddfellows Hall. He also built an Oriental Mount Zion Chapel but this has since been demolished. Today the Egyptian building is a social club with an apartment block built alongside. The column was to have a statue of George IV at the top, but he was an unpopular king and the funds never did become available!

The Pavilion and Fountain, Devonport Park, 1926. The park was laid out in 1858, and covered 37 acres of land. The park pavilion, near the park entrance in Paradise Road, is of an interesting design with the Devonport coat of arms at the top of the building. Refreshments could be obtained there, and it provided accommodation for the park keeper.

Devonport Park and Bandstand, photographed from the pavilion, c. 1920. The pretty fountain is in the foreground, with a gardener in the bushes, and we are looking towards Tamar Terrace, Portland Place and Milne Place, in Stoke. You can see the bandstand and the circular path around the top of the park known as the 'Oval'. During the war American troops had billets in the park. After the war a new road, Park Avenue, was built from Albert Road, across the park, to meet Chapel Street.

Devonport Park and the Hamoaze, 1906. Another view from the pavilion but looking left towards the Royal Dockyard and the Hamoaze. In the centre is the Doris Memorial. In the distance may be seen Albert Gate, foundry chimneys, a shearleg crane, ships 'up the trot' (in reserve), and Torpoint, Wilcove, and Saltash.

The Doris Memorial, 1908. The gun was captured from the Boers in the Battle of Paardeberg, in February 1900, during the Boer War. It was erected here by the officers and men of HMS *Doris* in memory of their shipmates who lost their lives in that campaign.

Prior & Son, Stoke tobacconist and newsagents, Tuesday 14 October 1913. Mr Prior, with his more fashionable son, and little daughter, gaze impassively at the photographer. The newspaper billboards show the date. The main news item is of a burning Atlantic liner, the *Volturno*, with pictures of the vessel. The *Western Morning News* adds an item on Sylvia Pankhurst and carries local news about Plymouth council and a tramway extension. I like the multitude of detail in this picture, like the advertisements: 'Nectar Tea', 'Lyons Tea', 'Campbell Dyers', 'Sunlight Soap', 'Stephens Ink', 'Cadbury's Chocolate', and 'Rowntree's Pastilles and Clear Gums'. In the right-hand window are jars of Tucketts sweets, other sweets and boxes of chocolates. In the window on the left are picture postcards, games such as draughts, books, photographs, birthday cards, pens, and items on cards – hair-slides, and so on. There is also a reflection over the word 'Prior', above the doorway, that shows the words 'Public Telephone', from a box positioned across the road.

Torpoint Ferry on the Devonport side, *c.* 1930. The army have been using the target range at Tregantle Fort and soldiers stream off the ferry with their rifles and horse-drawn gun carriages. A bull-nosed Morris and an open-topped Austin 7 await their turn to disembark. Pottery Quay is over on the right, and some sleek-looking Navy destroyers are in harbour. This design of ferry was just before my time, but is very similar to the ferries I knew as a youth. The captain then had a little 'driver's cabin' at each end of the craft, but here he seems to look out of a porthole in the front. As apprentices in the 1940s we caught the 6.30am ferry (if we were lucky) and entered the dockyard through Albert Gate to clock in before 7am. In the evening we had a snack in the canteen outside St Levan's Gate and went to night school from 6 to 9pm. What with various social diversions afterwards, I usually managed to board the 11.15pm ferry to Torpoint and went to sleep in the cabin, only to wake up at 2am – on the Devonport side!

Royal Albert Gate, *c.* 1904, with the 'Dockyardies' streaming out on time. This grand entrance to Keyham Dockyard was designed by Mr Scamp of the Admiralty's Department of Works and became known as the Albert Gate. Shearleg cranes and a foundry chimney can be seen inside the yard. The gate was closed for the last time on 4 September 1966 and the clock was moved to the right-hand tower. The left-hand tower was then demolished, the gateway walled up and a new gateway built part way up Albert Road. A massive frigate refitting complex now looms up behind the clock tower, looking like something from outer space.

Royal Albert Gate and Park, *c.* 1904. This view shows the little park on the left and a fruit and vegetable cart outside the gate. In later years there was a newspaper man and a man selling Ivor Dewdney's pasties. Workmen are digging a hole in the pavement and, as usual, everyone looks on.

St Levan's Gate, *c.* 1906. This is another dockyard gate further along Keyham Road at its junction with St Levan's Road. It appears to be lunch time with a lady and a boy selling food from baskets, while dockyard workers stand around idly. The man in the middle of the road, in a bowler hat, looks like a dockyard chargeman! The bell-tower is for in- and out-muster and a dockyard police building and chargemen's offices are behind the dockyard wall on the right. A ship's mast appears in the gateway, from a ship in No. 4 Basin. The tram, advertising Isaac Luke & Son, is moving off up Saltash Road towards the R.N. Barracks. It was much like this in the 1940s when I worked on HMS *Terrible* (18,000 tons), later HMAS *Sydney*. At lunch time we left the dockyard by St Levan's Gate to buy pasties and sausage rolls from the Criterion Bakery across the road.

Tram No. 15 in St Levan's Road, *c.* 1905. Note the gasometers at the bottom of Milehouse Hill and the display of washing in the back gardens of Alexandra Terrace. The area behind the railings is now occupied by a garage and the local social security offices. The tram sign shows Morice Square as the destination, and the driver and the conductor pose with studied nonchalance for the photographer, with their quaint vehicle on the wrong side of the road! Perhaps it's a Monday morning, and they are at the terminus ready to move off across the road, and on to Morice Square?

St Paul's Church, Morice Square, Devonport, 1907. St Paul's Church was among many designed by J. Piers St Aubyn. The foundation stone was laid on 25 July 1849 and the church was consecrated on 22 April 1851. Its grand spire was 104 ft high. The church was destroyed during the Blitz of 1941. This pretty, cobbled square was the tram terminus.

R.N. Engineering College, Keyham, 1902. This impressive building was sited in Keyham Road between Royal Albert and St Levan's Gates. It was opened in 1880 for training Engineering Officers for the Royal Navy. The R.N. Engineering College at Manadon was subsequently developed to do this work and this building was demolished in 1985.

Royal Naval Barracks, Devonport, 1911. These barracks were first occupied on 4 June 1889, and named HMS *Vivid*. The establishment then consisted of two main blocks, a drill shed, and the Commodore's house. The clock tower was added in 1896. The name was changed to HMS *Drake* on 25 January 1934.

H.E. Butler's shop, corner of Ryder Road and Freemantle Place, Stoke, *c.* 1905. Harriet Elizabeth Butler (née Organ) stands in the doorway holding a cabbage. She was my wife's great grandmother and was born in Redruth in 1854. Harriet was brought up in Charlestown and, at a young age, went into service and became a children's nanny. She subsequently married Joseph Butler, came to Plymouth and started in business in Ryder Road. It's a lovely old corner shop with adverts everywhere. There are groceries and sweets in the windows, and also theatre and cinema notices. Harry Korris stars at the Grand in *Don't Worry*, and at the Palladium they are showing Charlie Chaplin in *The Floor Walker*. There is also a bill advertising a 'Whist Tournament and Dance at St Mark's Schoolroom': a little reminder of those days before television. In more recent years the shop has been converted into a private dwelling house.

A Herbert Hotel Outing, Herbert Street, Stoke, *c*. 1948. The Herbert Hotel regulars are about to set off for an inter-pub darts match, and I remember going on one, years ago. Harry Byrnes is on the right in the bus doorway and Rene Byrnes, his wife, is hidden behind a lady on the other side. It's the team and supporters, and I wonder where they are going? Perhaps the lady in front with the bouquet of flowers is the organizer? They are all looking forward to a good evening, and a sing-song on the way home.

Tram No. 88 at Milehouse, 1929. The word 'Special' on the tram sign could mean that this is a football special awaiting the crowds coming out of Home Park during Argyle's promotion-winning year. For the more fanciful, it could be a ghostly 'Marie Celeste' tram condemned to rumble around without a soul on board. The location is Milehouse corner. The Britannia Pub is in the background, the Embassy Ballroom behind, and the houses in Tavistock Road (now Milehouse Road) are on the left.

The launch of battleship HMS *King Edward VII*, by the Prince and Princess of Wales (later King George V and Queen Mary), 23 July 1903. The top view is from Cremyll. The massive 16,350 ton battleship comes down the slipway at South Yard, with the training ship HMS *Impregnable* on the right accompanied by two wooden hulks. The bottom view shows the ship and the Hamoaze with that charming old tug, and a floating audience in attendance. This was the heyday of shipbuilding in Devonport Dockyard with proud launchings of some of the navy's mammoth-size ships. HMS *Queen* (15,000 tons) had been launched by King Edward VII and Queen Alexandra on 8 March 1902; they also laid the keel of HMS *King Edward VII* at that time. Both ships, *Queen* and *King Edward VII*, were designed by Sir William White KCB, a Devonport Dockyard apprentice who rose to become one of our greatest naval architects. Many more ships followed: *Minotaur* (14,600 tons) in 1906, *Collingwood* (19,200 tons) in 1908, *Lion* (26,350 tons) in 1910, *Warspite* (30,600 tons) in 1913, and *Royal Oak* (29,150 tons) in 1914. However, I expect that HMS *Exeter* (8,390 tons), launched in 1929, is best remembered because of its Devonport associations and its exploits at the Battle of the River Plate.

Mutton Cove, 1911. It is so named because the little harbour is in the shape of a leg of mutton. In the nineteenth and early twentieth centuries there was work for watermen running day trips and taking sailors back to their ships and even smuggling. This was a busy little harbour then, with about twenty or thirty buildings including about four pubs. The oldest was the Mutton Cove Inn where William Horrell was the landlord in 1830. The wine merchants Saccone & Speed used some of the buildings as stores, and coal was discharged here for a local coal merchant. In the eighteenth century a ferry ran from Mutton Cove to Mount Edgcombe, instead of Devil's Point to Cremyll, because of the growing importance of Plymouth Dock. The ferry was moved to Admiral's Hard when the latter was completed in 1824. The dockyard was extended to alongside the cove, and inside the dockyard wall is 'King Billy', a figurehead from HMS *Royal William*. This was a 120-gun ship built at Pembroke Dock in 1833 and destroyed by fire in the Mersey in 1899. Today the little harbour is still there, but all the houses and pubs have disappeared.

Mount Wise, 1905. The Royal Clarence Baths, in the foreground, provided bathing facilities during the nineteenth century. Behind the baths stands the Admiral's Boathouse with its arched entrances, and to the left is Bullock Dock. The wall around the foreshore is part of the boundary wall of Devonport built by the Duke of Richmond; above it the duke built Richmond Walk. The Admiralty Telegraph Station is in the background with the statue of Lord Seaton nearby. Today a boatyard occupies the site of the Royal Clarence Baths, the Admiral's Boathouse is a roofless relic, and Bullock Dock has become the Mount Wise Swimming Baths, which were opened in 1924. The Admiralty Telegraph Station has been replaced by blocks of naval married quarters, and Lord Seaton's statue has been removed to Seaton Barracks.

Admiralty House, Mount Wise, c. 1910. The house was built in 1795 and was the home of the Port Admiral for 140 years. On 9 June 1935 the then Commander in Chief, Admiral Sir Richard Ernle-Erle-Drax, moved to Government House, which is nearby across the parade, and that became Admiralty House. The original Admiralty House then became Hamoaze House, the administrative centre for the navy. In 1966 it became the headquarters of the Plymouth group of Royal Marines.

Scott Memorial, Mount Wise, *c.* 1925. This memorial commemorates Robert Falcon Scott, the Antarctic explorer who died tragically with his team on expedition in 1910. He was born on 6 June 1868 at Outlands, Milehouse, and was one of the most famous Plymothians of this century. The memorial was unveiled on 10 August 1925 by G.W.R. Royds, Commodore of the R.N. Barracks (a member of a previous Scott expedition). The bronze statue represents Courage, supported by Devotion and crowned by Immortality, while Fear, Death and Despair are trampled underfoot. Portraits of Scott, Oates, Wilson, Bowers, and Evans are in the bronze medallions. Note that the low decorative railings had not yet been installed. The Admiralty Telegraph Station is seen on the left. It provided direct morse-code communications with ships and London, but, with the improved communications of the twentieth century, the role of the station declined and it was demolished in about 1952. The happy band of chubby children on the right catch the eye; oblivious of brave explorers, or wartime horrors to come, they play away.

Ha'penny Bridge, 1912. This is Stonehouse Bridge which joins Devonport and Stonehouse. Lord George Edgcumbe and Sir John St Aubyn were given permission by Act of Parliament to build this bridge and they employed John Smeaton to carry out the work, which was completed in 1773. Tollgates were built and pedestrians were charged a halfpenny to cross the bridge, hence the name Ha'penny Bridge. A horse with a cart was charged 2d, two horses with a cart was 3d, and so on. On 1 April 1924 the tolls were abolished. A Plymouth Breweries building stands on the Stonehouse side, and there's a houseboat in the foreground with underwear swinging in the breeze.

On Ha'penny Bridge, c. 1910. A Plymouth-bound tram is at the tollgate and the Prince Albert public house is seen in the distance.

STONEHOUSE &

MILLBAY

Millbay station, the Duke of Cornwall Hotel, and St James the Less Church, with Millbay

Park, c. 1907.

The Royal William Victualling Yard, Stonehouse, viewed from Mount Wise, 1908. The admiral's yacht, HMS *Livid*, is seen at moorings, with a covered bathing place offshore. Bullock Dock is in the foreground, and the Royal Clarence Baths are on the promontory in the mid-distance.

The Royal William Victualling Yard, Stonehouse, 1932. A similar view, but with Mount Wise Swimming Baths now in the foreground.

An engraving of Clarence Wharf Storehouse, Royal William Victualling Yard, 1832. The yard was named after King William IV, the sailor king. Sir John Rennie, a prominent architect and engineer, and son of the famous John Rennie who designed and built many great civil engineering works, was commissioned to build the victualling yard. It was completed in 1835 after ten years of planning and construction work. The layout included buildings for milling flour, baking bread (biscuit), brewing beer, slaughtering and storage of meat, and a cooperage. All this was to meet the needs of the Royal Navy. The victualling yard is recognized as an example of great nineteenth-century architecture with high-quality workmanship seen in even the smallest detail. There is a massive gateway, designed in the Graeco-Roman style, surmounted by a 13 ft high statue of King William IV, a range of elegant buildings in limestone and granite, with an attractive dock, and the imposing Clarence Stairs (shown in the engraving). These were intended to be a landing stage for royalty and VIPs arriving by sea. In 1830 the king knighted John Rennie for his work. Today the Royal William Victualling Yard is no longer required for victualling the Navy and its future is now in the hands of the Plymouth Development Corporation.

Royal Marine Barracks, Stonehouse, 1904. Work began on the construction of these barracks in 1781 and the marines moved into their new accommodation on 8 December 1783. This is a view of the entrance block from the parade ground inside the barracks. The grand twin-towered development was designed by Mr W. Hake and completed in 1867. The other side of the block fronts on to Durnford Street.

Royal Naval Hospital, Stonehouse, 1917. A view through the gateway of this eighteenth-century hospital. It was designed by Alexander Rovehead and William Robinson, and there are fifteen Georgian buildings laid out in lawns. Now, after over 200 years of service, the Ministry of Defence has closed the hospital and sold the site for redevelopment.

The Winter Villa, Devil's Point, *c.* 1905. The villa was built by the Earl of Mount Edgcumbe and completed in 1856. Isaac Foot senior owned the great house for a time, then it was sold to the Sisters of Nazareth for use as an orphanage in 1932 and renamed Nazareth House. One wing of the house was destroyed during the Blitz and a chapel was built on the site in the 1950s. The villa was demolished in 1976 and the present modern building replacing it provides a purpose-built old people's home and a small orphanage in this lovely position looking out over Plymouth Sound. In the foreground children are swimming by the slipway, and in the distance you have a glimpse of the Citadel, Smeaton's Tower, and the Promenade Pier.

Millbay Docks, showing the Outer Basin, 1908. On the far (east) side of the basin, Trinity Pier is on the left, Princess Royal Pier, with Brunel's Pontoon, is in the middle, and Millbay Pier is on the right. The boats are, probably, the tender *Smeaton*, delivering mail at Princess Pier, the paddle steamer *Cheshire*, alongside the pontoon, and the tender *Sir Richard Grenville*, at Millbay Pier. In 1901 the London & South Western Railway opened their Ocean Terminal at Millbay Docks, and the Ocean Terminal buildings and Ocean Mails' express can be seen on the dockside. The two-funnelled ship in the foreground is the G.W.R. cross-channel steamer *Antelope* (or possibly the *Lynx*), while in the distance can be seen Smeaton's Tower, the Citadel, and Mount Batten Tower.

Millbay Docks, 1907. This is a view through the entrance to the Inner Basin and shows the North Quay. In 1846 the Great Western Dock Company employed Isambard Kingdom Brunel to design and build the new docks. The Inner Basin was part of Brunel's original 1851 specification and was completed in February 1857. It is 1,250 ft by 400 ft and constructed with limestone and granite walls. In 1902 the entrance was repositioned further west and new lock gates, hydraulic equipment and a swing bridge installed.

Paddle steamers, Millbay Docks, *c.* 1905. The Millbrook Steamboat Company operated mainly from the Promenade Pier but their splendid paddle steamers *Hibernia* and *Brunel* sailed on river trips from the Brunel Pontoon in Millbay Docks, as shown here. The large steamship lines were at this time making Plymouth the first port of disembarkation on the eastward route from America because it saved a day or more on the journey. The ocean liners anchored in the Sound and tenders would meet them and deliver their passengers to the Ocean Terminal at Millbay Docks and on to a train bound for London. In the distance may be seen the old lifeboat house and slipway on the west side of the docks. The new docks designed by Brunel, with subsequent modifications, ensured that liner passenger and mail trade prospered for many years. Since 1972 the west side has been developed to become the Plymouth ferry port with roll-on roll-off (RORO) berths for ferries to Santander in Spain and to Roscoff in France. On the east side of Millbay Docks the liner and mail business has long ceased and the place has been transformed into a marina with stylish housing and yacht berths.

Millbay station, *c.* 1905. The South Devon Railway reached Plymouth in 1848 and Millbay station was opened on 4 April 1849. A rail connection to Millbay Docks was completed in 1850. Millbay remained Plymouth's main terminus until North Road station was opened on 28 March 1877. Millbay station was damaged by bombs during the 1941 Blitz on Plymouth and was closed to passenger traffic from 23 April that year. It continued to be used by goods trains and empty rolling stock until its final closure on 20 June 1966.

Duke of Cornwall Hotel, 1911. This fine ornate modern gothic building was completed in 1865 and is sited opposite Millbay station on Millbay Road. Together with the Albion Hotel (now the New Continental), built in the early 1870s, it provided accommodation for travellers using the new rail and sea terminus. It still stands at the junction with Citadel Road today.

Section Three

THE HOE &

CITADEL

The Drake and Armada Memorials, the Hoe, c. 1910.

Plymouth Hoe, from the Grand Hotel looking east; top picture, *c.* 1900; lower picture, *c.* 1950. Both views show Smeaton's Tower and the Citadel, with the Cattewater in the background. The one significant change to be seen in fifty years is the loss of the Victorian bandstand. I believe it was damaged during the Blitz and the iron was taken away for melting down for the war effort – together with our front railings!

The Hoe Promenade, 1908. This is a view from the Citadel looking west along the promenade towards Smeaton's Tower; the bandstand and the Grand Hotel are in the distance.

Unveiling the Naval War Memorial, 29 July 1924. Large crowds attended the unveiling of this memorial, which commemorates the sailors lost during the First World War. Now it also includes those who gave their lives during the Second World War. The tall obelisk has four buttresses with lions, and around its base are panels listing all those who fell in the various theatres of war. The Armada Memorial, which commemorates the defeat of the Spanish Armada in 1588, is shown on the right.

The Hoe and bandstand, *c*. 1904. A lovely photograph of preparations for a band concert on the Hoe. The stylish bandstand is nearly ready, the deckchairs have been put out and the crowd is starting to gather. This is the western side of the Hoe and the imposing early nineteenth-century houses on the right are (right to left) Elliott Terrace, the Grand Hotel and the Royal Western Yacht Club. Lord and Lady Astor once owned 3 Elliot Terrace, and they gave it to the city in 1964. In the middle of the picture is the Belvedere and Bull Ring, and on the left, the entrance to the Promenade Pier with West Hoe and West Hoe Pier. In the distance is Millbay Docks, Mount Wise and the Hamoaze.

Feu de joie, the Hoe, 22 June 1897. It is Queen Victoria's diamond jubilee and the crowds have gathered for the celebrations on the Hoe. There is a parade of horses and carriages, and the soldiers are lined up along Madeira Road for their rippling rifle-shot salute, with the Citadel and the Cattewater as a backdrop. The celebrations ended with a big bonfire on the Hoe in the evening.

The Hoe looking north, 1903. Through the trees you can just discern St Andrew's Church and the Guildhall in the city. A lady promenades in her long dress and there were sheep grazing on the Hoe at the turn of the century.

Strolling on the Hoe, 1912. An atmospheric picture of family groups arriving on the Hoe from Lockyer Street. There is the elegance of the group on the right, the busy lady with a pushchair, and the casual gait of the man on the left, with Drake's Memorial in the distance. This photograph must have been difficult to achieve (depth of focus, shutter speed and so on), and it is unfortunate that the pole is sticking out of the lady's head!

South African War Memorial, 1907. This obelisk was erected by Alfred Mosely in memory of Prince Schleswig-Holstein and the officers and men who fell during the Boer War, 1899–1902. The memorial was unveiled by Lady Buller in 1903 and still stands near the Citadel. In 1907 there was this splendid view over the old city to the Guildhall, Municipal Buildings, and St Andrew's Church.

Sitting on the Belvedere, *c*. 1904. A study of people relaxing in the sunshine on the Hoe. The camera inevitably attracts attention, even today, and individuals could not resist either a peep, or a disdainful stare, in our direction. In the background a band concert is in progress and the music drifts over on the breeze.

Having a lovely time on The Hoe, *c*. 1908. The photographer has caught them unawares this time, except for the straw-hatted 'doctor' with his gladstone bag in the foreground. Some people pay up and listen to the band in splendid deckchaired comfort behind the tarpaulin surrounding the bandstand. Others forsake a sight of the sweating tuba player and enjoy a free lounge on the grass, or stroll around eyeing up the talent!

Two views of Sir Francis Drake Bowling Green. The top photograph, *c.* 1903, shows bowlers in action, or gazing at the camera. The bottom photograph shows the view from the junction of Citadel Road and Lockyer Street, *c.* 1930. Observe the Naval War Memorial, and Armada and Drake Memorials in the distance. There is now a modern register office and a bowling pavilion on this side of the bowling green. Sir Francis Drake did not play his famous game of bowls on this site in 1588. It is thought that he played further to the east, possibly on ground where the Citadel is today.

Two views of the slopes of the Hoe, *c.* 1904. The top view, looking east, shows the fine three-tiered Belvedere, completed in 1892. The Bull Ring is at the bottom and bulls were baited here, before the practice was banned in 1815. Smeaton's Tower and the Bandstand are in the distance and there are large crowds in Hoe Road at the entrance to the Promenade Pier. The bottom photograph looks towards West Hoe with (right to left) Elliot Terrace, the Grand Hotel, and the Royal Western Yacht Club.

The Pier, Plymouth

Promenade Pier, with the Plymouth Breakwater in the distance, 1904. This large pier was opened on 29 May 1884 and was a prominent landmark with its waterside location, wrought-iron railings, domes, clock, and bright lights. Dances were very popular and there were promenade concerts, summer shows and afternoon teas with a trio playing in the background. At various times there was also roller skating, fishing competitions, acrobats, wrestling and boxing. Pleasure steamers and smaller craft departed from the pier for journeys up the local rivers and for boat trips to many locations. All this came to an end when the pier was destroyed by fire bombs in April 1941 during the height of the Blitz on Plymouth. The breakwater, on the horizon, is necessary to prevent south-westerly gales damaging shipping moored in the Sound. It was designed and built by John Rennie senior and Joseph Whidbey, and is nearly 3 miles south of the Hoe. It is positioned in the middle of the Sound and is about a mile long, leaving an eastern and western entrance to the harbour. The breakwater was built by dumping limestone, taken from a new quarry in Oreston, into the water in the designated area. The work was started in 1812 and officially completed in 1841. Sadly, John Rennie died in 1821 and his sons, John and George, completed the task. The lighthouse on the western end and the beacon on the eastern end were not completed until 1845. The separate fort in the centre of the breakwater was completed in 1860.

Promenade Pier, *c.* 1905, looking towards the Devon side of the Sound, with a view of the pier, Mount Batten Breakwater, Jennycliffe Bay, Staddon Heights and Bovisand Bay.

Promenade Pier and paddle steamer, 1907. The view is from Rusty Anchor of the paddle steamer *Alexandra* approaching West Hoe Pier, with the Promenade Pier and the Hoe in the distance.

Promenade Pier, Drake's Island, and Mount Edgcumbe, c. 1900. Sailing ships are passing and 'The Terrace' and Rusty Anchor are on the right. Drake's Island is on the left with Mount Edgcumbe in the distance. Drake's Island was known as St Michael's Island in the twelfth century. In the seventeenth century it was called St Nicholas Island and Sir Alexander Carew was its governor for Cromwell during the Civil War, when Plymouth was besieged by Royalists. He had doubts about his role and decided to change sides, but before he could act his servant gave him away, and he died on the Tyburn gibbet in London. In the nineteenth century large gun emplacements were built on the island because of fears of a French invasion. They were never required and this beautifully situated island has since been used for numerous ventures. The island is crown property and is now for sale.

Promenade Pier, the Hoe Bandstand and Hancock's Fair, 1907. In addition to the entertainment provided on the pier and bandstand, there was Hancock's Fair which set up at a number of sites in the district. Here the fair is in the quarry at West Hoe. There are roundabouts, helter-skelters, swings and sideshows – all the fun of the fair.

The Hoe, *c.* 1934. The large sea-water bathing pool at Tinside was opened on 2 October 1935 and the Promenade Pier was destroyed in the Blitz of April 1941. These two features only existed together, therefore, for less than six years. The Hoe foreshore was also being developed with limestone-fronted bathing houses, sun terraces, cliff paths, and promenade from about 1913 to 1935. Careful examination of this view shows that the bathing pool and surrounding structures are still in course of construction. The beach at Tinside is on the right while the Ladies' Bathing Place, which was opened in 1877, is to the left of the main pool. The Gentlemen's (or 'Shaggey') pool, opened in 1907, is just discernible this side of the pier. From right to left in the background are the Esplanade, Elliott Terrace, the Grand Hotel, and the Royal Western Yacht Club. The R.W.Y.C. was another prominent Hoe feature to be destroyed during the Blitz in 1941. It was later re-established on West Hoe Pier, seen on the left, and has now moved to new premises at Queen Anne's Marina outside Sutton Harbour.

Ladies' bathing place, *c.* 1902. Ladies enjoying their pool, with Mount Batten Breakwater in the background.

Regatta Day, *c.* 1905. The crowds have gathered along the Hoe front to see the rowing races. The local rowing clubs and naval establishments competed in the various competitions. If you rowed in a whaler, you probably couldn't sit down for a week! I remember best the yachting regattas, and competing in International Class dinghy racing in the Sound.

The Hoe and Smeaton's Tower from the Aquarium, 1936. The ice-cream vendors are busy at the junction of Hoe Road and Madeira Road, and Smeaton's Tower dominates the scene. John Smeaton was a famous civil engineer and he designed this lighthouse for the dreaded Eddystone rocks, some 14 miles south-west of Plymouth. He first produced the stonework onshore and then built his tower on the rocks, completing the task in 1759. By the mid-nineteenth century the rock on which the lighthouse stood became undermined by the sea, and James Douglass completed his replacement lighthouse on an adjacent rock in May 1882. Funds were raised to remove the hollow part of Smeaton's Tower and rebuild it on the Hoe, the stump remaining on the rock. The work was completed, and Smeaton's Tower was opened to the public in 1884.

Hoe Road, Elliot Terrace and the Grand Hotel, *c.* 1950. Note the gap to the left of the Grand Hotel, where the Royal Western Yacht Club stood before its destruction during the bombing. The cars, fondly remembered Morris 8 Series Es and Ford 10s, park along the road.

The Citadel and the Hoe, c. 1948. Charles II instructed John Grenville, Earl of Bath and Governor of Plymouth, to build this massive citadel in 1665, ostensibly to strengthen the defences of Plymouth. Since the city had supported the Parliamentary cause, and withstood a Royalist siege during the Civil War, the king may have been ensuring that they couldn't do it again. The Citadel incorporated an existing fort to form the star shape seen here. The top of the Main Gateway with a guardroom is on the right. Across the square, in the centre of the picture, is a lead statue of George II. It stands in front of the officers' mess and the accommodation block. Just in front of this building (and obscured from view) is the royal chapel of St Katherine-upon-the-Hoe. This was rebuilt in 1845 and is still in regular use. Since 1896 the Citadel has been garrisoned mainly by the Royal Artillery and it is now an ancient monument. Note the bathing pool on the left, and the foundations of the bombed pier. In the distance can be seen Millbay Docks with the inner and outer basins.

Tinside swimming pool, *c*. 1945. Everyone is having a lovely time in the pool, with Drake's Island and Mount Edgcumbe in the distance.

Main gateway, the Citadel, 1913. This is the most striking architectural feature of the Citadel, and was probably designed by Sir Thomas Fitz, an associate of Sir Christopher Wren. The gateway bears the royal coat of arms at the top, and the arms of John Grenville, Earl of Bath (son of Sir Beville Grenville) over the archway. Above the arms is a niche, which may have been intended for a statue of Charles II, but now contains four cannonballs. Originally the main gateway was approached via an outer gateway and a drawbridge.

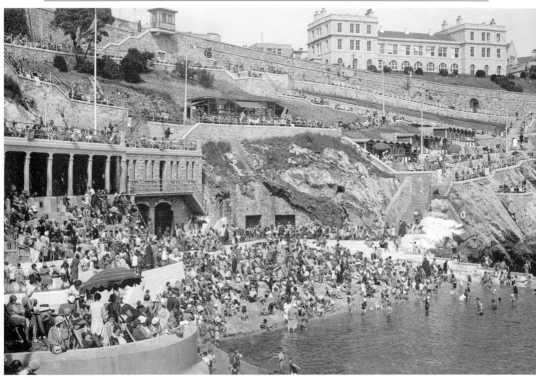

Bathing at Tinside, 1936. The little beach alongside the Tinside swimming pool is crowded with people who prefer the beach to the pool. They have a view of famous Plymouth Sound, with perhaps a liner or naval shipping passing by. Maybe there's a Regatta with dozens of yachts racing about. There's time for a chat and everyone seems to be enjoying themselves, but very few take their clothes off. What a difference now! The building in the background was constructed in 1887, and houses the famous Plymouth Marine Biological Laboratory, and the Aquarium.

A TOUR OF OLD

PLYMOUTH

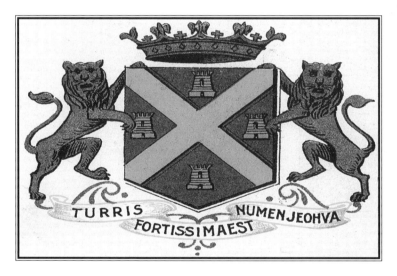

Plymouth coat-of-arms, c. 1910

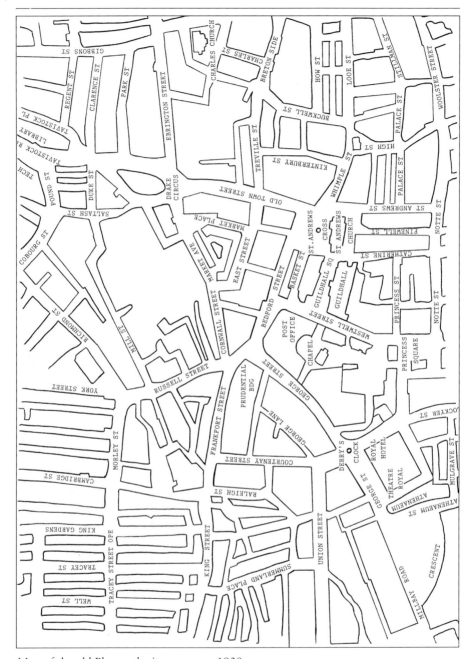

Map of the old Plymouth city centre, *c.* 1930.

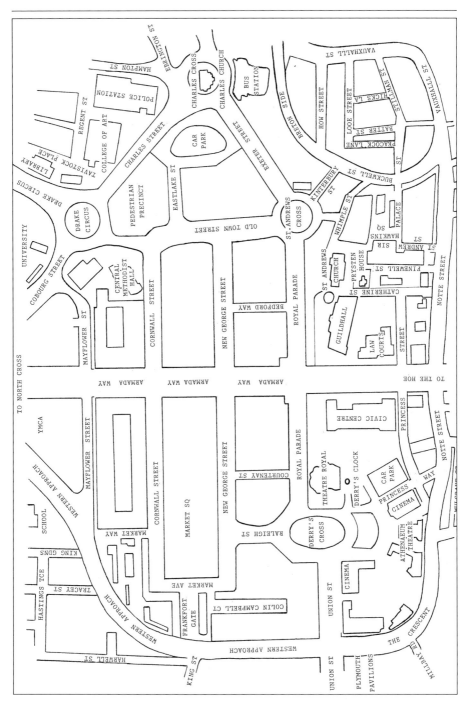

Map of the new Plymouth city centre.

St Andrew's Cross, *c.* 1905. We start our tour of old Plymouth from St Andrew's Cross and Gardens. The impressive Yogge Tower of St Andrew's Church looms alongside, and the Guildhall and Municipal Buildings are in the background. These are buildings of delicacy and colour, with many lofty turrets and pinnacles.

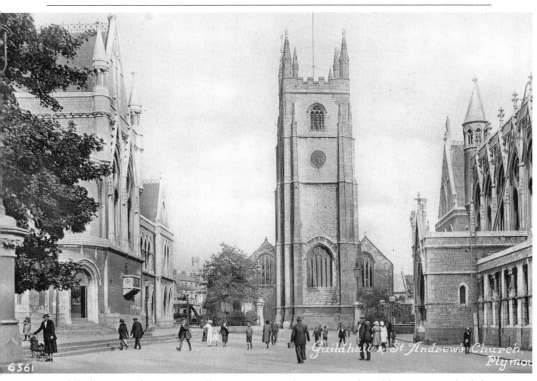

Guildhall Square from Westwell Street, 1932. The Municipal Buildings are on the left, St Andrew's Church in the centre and the Guildhall on the right. The architects for the Guildhall and the Municipal Buildings were Alfred Norman and James Hine, and the builders were Benjamin Call and John Pethick. The buildings were constructed of beautiful local materials, such as Dartmoor granite and Plymouth limestone, and the architecture was French Gothic. The tower at the south-west corner of the Guildhall rose over 190 ft high and life-size statues of Edward I, Drake, Hawkins, Frobisher and others were placed at the apex of each gable of the Guildhall, the law courts and the council chamber. The six panels on each side of the porch represented painting, sculpture, astronomy, mechanics, architecture, music, commerce, plenty, law, peace, war, and religion. The Municipal Buildings were opened on 16 April 1873 by the mayor, John Kelly, and the Guildhall was opened on 13 August 1874 by the Prince of Wales. Both buildings were gutted on 21 March 1941 during the Blitz on Plymouth. Plymouth Council decided to demolish the Municipal Buildings to make way for Royal Parade, but in October 1950 the decision was taken to restore the Guildhall to its former glory. It was re-opened on 24 September 1959 by Field Marshal The Viscount Montgomery of Alamein.

Plymouth Guildhall from St Andrew's Church, 1906. Note the statues at the apex of each gable, and the tower in the south-west corner. The Justices' Court was on the left, the Guildhall in the middle, and the Law Courts at the far end. Note also the entrance to the square from this end, and the general post office in the distance.

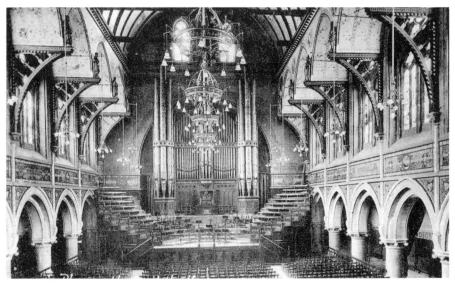

The Great Hall in the Guildhall, *c.* 1926. The massive grandeur of the Great Hall (146 ft long, 58 ft wide and 70 ft high) that seated 2,600 people. The concert organ was at the west end of the hall and was one of the finest in the country. The fourteen stained-glass windows, seen down both sides, illustrate important events in the history of the city.

Guildhall Square from Westwell Street, 1902. The Municipal Buildings are on the left with the Guildhall on the right and St Andrew's Church in the background. Note the entrance from Westwell Street. The statue on the left is of Alfred Rooker, a Liberal, former mayor, and Orator of Plymouth Council. Tory members of the council made sure that the statue was placed as near as possible to the public toilets! Politics is a dirty business.

Guildhall Square from St Andrew's Church, 1906. The Guildhall is on the left, the general post office in the centre and the Municipal Buildings on the right. The Municipal Buildings comprised a council chamber in the centre, with municipal offices at each end. The general post office was built of Portland stone, and opened in 1884. It is not actually a part of the square but is on the other side of Westwell Street. The building was destroyed on 21 March 1941 during the Blitz and was demolished for the building of Armada Way.

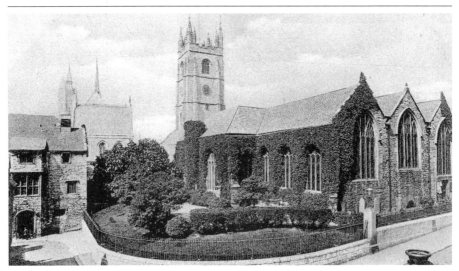

St Andrew's Church and Prysten House, *c*. 1905. St Andrew's Church is a fifteenth-century church with nineteenth-century additions. It is a typical Devon church with beautiful granite arcades. Its Yogge Tower is so called because Thomas Yogge, a merchant and mayor of Plymouth, provided the funds for the building of this sturdy tower. The church was restored by John Foulston in 1826 and restored again by Sir Gilbert Scott in 1875. Then, during the Blitz on 21 March 1941, the church was gutted, with only the damaged walls and the Yogge Tower left standing. The single word *Resurgam* (I will rise again) was placed above the north porch and the church left roofless for a period. Then the church was indeed rebuilt and a festival of re-consecration held from 30 November to 8 December 1957. The Prysten House, on the left, was owned by Thomas Yogge in the fifteenth century. In 1884 the house became The Abbey stores and was well known for its hams, salt fish, and so on. It was restored in 1928, survived the Blitz and is still there, around the back of the church.

Interior of St Andrew's Church, *c*. 1905.

St Andrew's Church and Cross, *c.* 1910. St Andrew's Cross was unveiled on 30 May 1895. It had three tiers of stone minarets topped with a bronze cross, which was believed to have been cast during the reign of Queen Elizabeth I. The monument was damaged during the Blitz and had to be dismantled. Unfortunately explosives were used and the monument was so badly broken that it could not be re-erected after the war. Parts of the edifice were incorporated into the north-facing wall of the Guildhall when it was rebuilt. The Municipal Buildings are on the right.

Bateman's Corner, 1939. A very familiar sight to those who remember sitting in St Andrew's Cross Gardens long ago. From the left you can see a bus approaching up Catherine Street past the Municipal Buildings, and buses in Basket Street, leading to Westwell Street, then Bedford Street with the Prudential Building at the end, and Spooner's Corner on the right. Note that the tramlines go from Spooner's Corner, down Basket Street, and turn left into Westwell Street.

Westwell Street, the general post office and the Guildhall, 1919. We are looking along Westwell Street. The general post office is on the right and the entrances to Basket Street and Guildhall Square on the left, with the Guildhall tower in the distance. The YMCA moved into their premises on the corner of Westwell Street and Bedford Street in 1887, and then moved to Old Town Street in 1920. Westwell Street was named after the West Well which was located here.

Basket Street, looking towards St Andrew's Cross, *c.* 1930. The Municipal Buildings are on the right. Trams strewn with adverts are passing, and this racy MG sports-car, registration FJ5766, steams towards us through the 'canyon', whilst stylish ladies queue for a tram. A touch of nostalgia, of good times, if you had a job.

BEDFORD STREET, PLYMOUTH

Bedford Street, *c.* 1930. A view from Spooner's Corner up through Bedford Street to the Prudential Building. The Prudential Assurance Company built their offices on the site of the old Globe Theatre. It was near the old Frankfort (or West) Gate, one of the original town gates which had given access to Devonport before the building of Union Street in 1815. This is an interesting view of a pre-war Plymouth street with an increasing road-traffic problem. Note the detail and stonework on the Spooner's Corner building. The Tuckett's shop, in the bottom right corner, sold sweets made in their well-known local confectionery business of E. Tuckett and Son; many shops in Plymouth sold Tuckett's sweets.

Bedford Street, *c*. 1910. At this end of Bedford Street the road divides, with George Street on the left, Frankfort Street straight ahead, and Russell Street on the right. The large and impressive Prudential Building was constructed of granite and glazed red marble and opened in 1904. It was damaged by fire bombs during the Blitz but the building did not receive a direct hit from high explosives. After the war the building remained there like a large, florid Edwardian lady, with a crumpled hat and feet slightly out of line, until the demolition men knocked her down in January 1951. On the left is Shandon Carpets, and Goodbody's Restaurant, while on the right is Webb & Son Leather Goods.

Bedford Street from the Prudential Building, *c*. 1904. There are plenty of people shopping, but no cars or trams. On the left are Dingle's, Underwood's, Blanchard's, Webb & Son, the Borough Arms, John Yoe's and Spooner's at the far end. On the block leading to Westwell Street are Perkin's Hosiers and Snell Tobacconist.

George Street, with horse-drawn vehicles and crowds milling about in the sunshine, *c*. 1903. The Prudential Building is on the right-hand side. Notice how the street bends to the right at the bottom.

George Street, 1906. This is the view from the bend in the street to Derry's Clock at the other end. Observe the advertisements: Parker & Smith pianos, Maton Tailors, and Cousins Chiropodist.

Derry's Clock, *c.* 1930. William Derry presented this clock to the city in 1862, during his period as mayor. Plymouth Corporation then provided the stone tower to support the clock and installed it in this location. The gilded ironwork was neglected, however, and the drinking fountains remained dry. It became known as the 'four-faced deceiver' because the four faces seemed to show different times. Some refute this, saying that the difference is due to viewing the hands of the clock from different angles. Derry's Clock became a popular meeting place for friends and courting couples having a night in town. Behind the clock-tower is George Street, and on the right is Lloyds Bank. This was previously the Wilts & Dorset Bank and is now a pub. The corner on the left leads to Courtenay and Union Streets; the buildings carry large advertisements for Tuckett's sweets and Player's Navy Cut tobacco. Dunn & Co., hat makers' shop is below. Previously this block had been the London & South Western Railway Offices with those words emblazoned around the hoarding at the top.

Derry's Clock, Theatre Royal and Royal Hotel, *c.* 1905. Looking from George Street this time, the Wilts & Dorset Bank (later Lloyds) is on the left with the large block housing the hotel and theatre behind the clock-tower. Lockyer Street is on the left and George Street continues past the theatre and then becomes Millbay Road. John Foulston designed and built the Royal Hotel (on the left) and the Theatre Royal, on the site of a cherry garden; the work was completed in 1813. The Royal Hotel was destroyed during the Blitz of April 1941.

Royal Hotel and Derry's Clock, 1903. A view down Lockyer Street towards Derry's Clock with the pillared portico of the hotel on the left. Coaches and horses, and trams provide the transport, with a horse and cart delivering provisions.

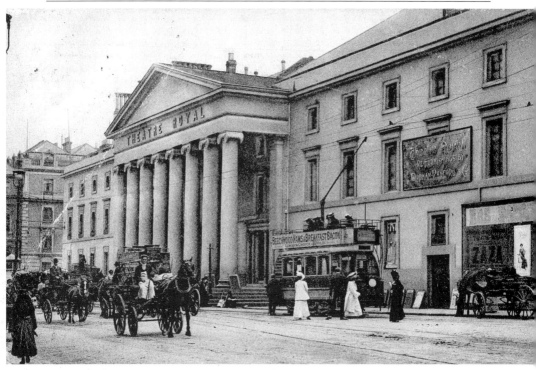

Theatre Royal, 1903. Foulston designed and built this noble, pillared building for the municipal council. The theatre opened in 1813 and seated 1,192 patrons. The Theatre Royal, the Royal Hotel and the Athenaeum, at the end of George Street, had all been designed by John Foulston and formed a group of fine buildings for Plymouth. The notice on the wall states 'Re-furnishings by Popham Radford & Co.', and the tram plys from Peverell Park to the Theatre. Surprisingly, in 1936 the municipal council decided to close the Theatre Royal and sell the site to a cinema organization. The theatre was pulled down and a cinema opened the following year. It was initially called the Royal Cinema and survived the Blitz. In 1954 the name reverted to the Theatre Royal when there were stage productions as well as films. In 1958 it was renamed the ABC Cinema. The Athenaeum was destroyed during the bombing but it was rebuilt on a site nearby.

Union Street, *c.* 1904. This is the Plymouth end of Union Street, around the corner from Derry's Clock. It was built by John Foulston to unite the three towns of Plymouth, Stonehouse, and Plymouth Dock (Devonport in 1824), and was completed in 1815. Before this date the area had been marshland at the head of a creek which ran down to Millbay Docks. This view shows the road thronged with shoppers in the late afternoon. The shops on the left include Albert Pengelly, W.G. Capps, Oliver's, and Wright's Hairdressers. Down the right-hand side is William's tea shop, and the Posada American Cocktail Bar. Almost everyone wears a hat and there are family groups with prams and push-chairs. The dome of the Palace Theatre can be seen in the far distance, and, just beyond the railway bridge is Andrew's Picture House, which was later replaced by the Gaumont Palace in 1931. The bars, dance halls, and theatres of Union Street made it a celebrated night-time venue, particularly for 'Jolly Jack' when in port. Nearly all Union Street, from here to the Octagon, was wiped out in 1941.

Union Street, *c.* 1908. The policeman, on point duty during a quiet daytime period, had a much busier time at night. A railway bridge was erected across Union Street in 1840, to carry the South Devon Railway line to the Millbay terminus, then this replacement bridge was erected in the 1890s. With the demise of Millbay station the bridge became redundant, and it was finally removed in 1974.

The Palace Theatre, *c.* 1905. The theatre was opened in 1898 as a large music hall, and, after a few months, was severely damaged by fire. It re-opened in July 1899 with its façade panels depicting Sir Oswald Brierley's celebrated Armada pictures. I remember the terrific shows they used to present, such as 'Paint Your Wagon' and 'South Pacific'. All those lovely songs, and the male-voice choir strewn across the stage, belting out 'There ain't nothing like a dame'!

St Andrew's Cross and Spooner's Corner, 1912. We have returned from Union Street to St Andrew's Cross. Now the view is towards Spooner's Corner and Old Town Street. Spooner's Corner was a landmark, and Old Town Street is one of the oldest parts of Plymouth. The whole area was devastated during the bombing in 1941.

Old Town Street and Spooner's Corner, 1912. Continuing around Spooner's Corner, Spooner's departmental store occupies the corner position and the whole block on the left. At the end of the street is Drake's Circus with an advertisement for Bovril at the top. Joseph Spooner had started his business in Whimple Street in the early nineteenth century, but by 1890 it occupied this site, and had already experienced disastrous fires in 1902 and 1910. Treville Street is the first turning on the right, and that leads to Breton Side. Old Town Street dates back to Elizabethan times, and Treville Street was named after the merchant Richard Treville. The name Breton Side is derived from the Breton invasion of 1403 when thirty French ships and 1,200 soldiers sailed into the Cattewater and set fire to 600 houses before being repelled.

Drake's Circus and Ebrington Street, *c.* 1905. The Drake's Circus block is on the left and it survived the war. Tavistock Road is to the left, and Ebrington Street is straight ahead. A detour down Ebrington Street takes us to Charles Church in Green Street.

Charles Church, *c.* 1920. This church was built before and after the 1643–6 Royalist siege of Plymouth. Its most famous vicar was Robert Hawker (1784–1827), who filled the church with vast congregations. In 1787 he founded the Household of Faith, the first Plymouth Sunday School and one of the first in the country. Hawker also opened an orphanage and school for the destitute. His grandson, Robert Stephen Hawker (1804–75) became the colourful vicar of Morwenstow church in North Cornwall. He was also a poet and wrote the words to the Cornish anthem *Trelawny*. Charles Church was gutted during the Blitz on Plymouth in 1941.

Tavistock Road, *c.* 1904, looking up Tavistock Road from Drake's Circus with Park and Clarence Streets on the right, and Duke Street to the left. At the top is Plymouth Technical & Art College.

Plymouth Technical & Art College, *c.* 1900. The 'Old Tech' once faced the Central Library. The foundation stone was laid in 1889 and the college opened in 1892. It was built to commemorate Queen Victoria's jubilee of 1887 and there were decorative panels along the front of the building with the words 'Victoria Jubilee Memorial Science Art and Technical Schools' and coats of arms. In 1951 the new college was started in Glanville Street, and in July 1966 this old building was demolished to make way for road widening at Drake's Cross roundabout. On the left is the Harvest Home Hotel with its name on the hanging lantern. It was built in about 1830 as a coaching house, with a stable yard at the rear, and was a local landmark and meeting place. In November 1964 it was demolished for new development.

Cobourg Street, 1938. A short detour to the left from the Harvest Home leads, via Pounds Road, to Cobourg Street. The old Public Central School, opened in 1927, stands on the right and the road wends its way towards North Road station. Today the houses on the left have been demolished, and Cobourg Street now leads to North Cross.

Plymouth Museum, Art Gallery and Central Library, Tavistock Road, *c.* 1910. This grand neo-classical building was designed by Thornley and Rooke and was erected in 1907–10. It has a granite base with moulded stone dressings and ashlar limestone walls. This end of the building, with the grand entrance, houses a museum and art gallery and the far end houses the library. The library was bombed on 22 April 1941, and many important books and documents were destroyed. A temporary library was opened on 9 August 1941 in a wing of the museum. The original library premises were redesigned to retain the original façade but include modern requirements, and the new Central Library opened on 22 February 1956.

Tavistock Road, *c.* 1903. This is beyond the library and looking towards Mutley Plain. Sherwell Congregational Church on the left was built in 1864 to replace a church at Norley Street, off Ebrington Street. Further up on the left is Drake's Reservoir, and St Mathias' Church is in the distance, on the right.

Drake's Reservoir, Tavistock Road, 1910. In 1591 Sir Francis Drake completed his scheme to bring fresh water to Plymouth via a 17 mile open leat. Then, when iron pipes were introduced in the nineteenth century, piped water supplies were taken to a number of small reservoirs at different elevations. Drake's Reservoir was the first to be completed in the late 1840s. Reservoirs then followed at Crownhill in 1851, Hartley in 1862, and Roborough in 1885. Here we look down on to the reservoir, with its elegant arches and pretty gardens, from a building across Tavistock Road.

The Blind Institution, North Hill, Tavistock Road, c. 1905. This is a view looking towards Mutley Plain. The foundation stone was laid by the Earl of Mount Edgcumbe on 19 April 1876, and the building opened on 26 October 1977. James Gale, blind himself, and other prominent individuals made great efforts to establish the Blind Institution. Work for the blind continued here until 1964 when the institution moved to Stonehouse. This building is now part of Plymouth High School for Girls.

Mutley Plain from North Hill, 1908. A quiet time with just a few trams and horse-drawn vehicles passing through Mutley Plain. The distinctive bulk of Mutley Baptist Church is on the left, where it still remains, and the Co-operative Society (est. 1880) is on the right.

Mutley Plain, 1904. Two more views of Mutley Plain, with the spire of Mutley Methodist Church prominently displayed. The church was built in 1881 and it could hold a congregation of 1,000, with room for 400 scholars in the basement. The church was demolished a few years ago. Observe the many small shops in the top photograph: Ahern's Fish Supplies, Millbay Laundry, Millington's and Harding Furnishings. In the lower picture an elegant lady walks down a tree-lined avenue, with Mutley Baptist Church on the horizon. A quiet and almost rural scene in those days before the coming of the motor car, and a good place to end our tour.

REBIRTH OF PLYMOUTH CITY CENTRE

The Guildhall and St Andrew's Church, c. 1965.

George Street after the Blitz, 1941. A view across devastated George Street with broken and burnt-out buildings everywhere. The Prudential Building is on the right, with the old *Western Morning News* building and the Odeon Cinema in the centre. The Co-operative Society building, on the corner of Frankfort and Courtenay Streets, is in the background on the left.

Westwell, Bedford, and Basket Streets after the Blitz, 1941. Here we look along Westwell Street with the burnt-out general post office building in the left foreground. The block between Bedford and Basket Streets on the right has been destroyed, together with the buildings along Bedford Street. East Street and Market Avenue are in the background.

Royal Parade at the end of 1947. During fifty-nine air-raids on the city of Plymouth, between June 1940 and April 1944, both Plymouth and Devonport shopping centres were virtually destroyed. In these attacks 1,172 civilians were killed and over 3,000 injured. Some 3,900 houses were destroyed and 18,400 others seriously damaged. The most devastating raids were during March and April 1941. The plan for the rebuilding of Plymouth was devised by the City Engineer, Paton Watson, and consultant Sir Patrick Abercrombie in 1943. Work started in March 1947, and Royal Parade was opened by King George VI on 29 October 1947. In this photograph the Guildhall is on the left, and the Municipal Buildings have been demolished to make way for the new Royal Parade. The Prudential Building stands on the right with the Odeon Cinema behind. The remains of George Street run diagonally across from in front of the Prudential Building to the left of the picture, and although Basket and Westwell Streets have gone, a small remnant of Bedford Street is visible on the right. The Co-operative Society building is at the bottom of Royal Parade, and Union Street is in the distance.

Royal Parade, 1948. This view is from the Levy and Sloggett building on Derry's Cross at the western end of Royal Parade. The pavement on the right has now been completed. The flagstaff, with the bronze cylinder at its base in the form of Drake's drum, was unveiled by King George VI in October 1947. Cars are still parked in the remains of the old George Street, outside the Nissen-hut shops which many well-known local firms used as temporary accommodation. This area later became the site of the new civic centre, with the new Theatre Royal adjacent at this end of Royal Parade. Over on the left are the old Courtenay and Frankfort Streets; this area is still being prepared for the buildings on the north side of Royal Parade, and the laying out of roads parallel with Royal Parade.

Two views of Royal Parade, early 1960s. Modern buildings have been erected in Portland stone on the north side of Royal Parade. Dingle's opened on 1 September 1951, the Plymouth Co-operative Society building on 27 December 1952, and the Pearl building on 9 January 1953. The south side of Royal Parade still has temporary shops, and awaits later development. Behind the shops on the north side of Royal Parade, the parallel New George Street and Cornwall Street are taking shape. The old Prudential Building was demolished in 1951 to make way for Armada Way.

Spooner's Corner after the bombing, March 1941. This view is from the tower of St Andrew's Church. It shows the top of St Andrew's Cross in the foreground and the shattered remains of Spooner's departmental store, and all the other buildings at this end of Old Town Street (see pages 75 and 76).

The destruction in Old Town Street, March 1941. This is around the corner from the view above and we are looking towards Drake's Circus with its familiar Bovril sign. On the right is a tailor's shop on the corner with Treville Street. Old Town Street and Spooner's Corner were destroyed in the same air raid on 21 March 1941.

Old Town Street and Charles Church, *c.* 1946. The ruined buildings have been flattened and cleared away, to leave an eerie landscape. Old Town Street is curving across the bottom left corner of the picture, and Treville Street runs off to the right. Surprisingly, the old building housing the tailor's shop (see previous picture) is still on the corner, with the Pearl Assurance offices alongside. On this side of Treville Street is the battered Spread Eagle public house. The spire of Charles Church is prominent in the background. The church was gutted during the bombing; it was made safe and retained in its bombed condition as a memorial in the middle of Charles Cross. St Jude's Church can also be seen in the distance.

Old Town Street, *c.* 1962. This photograph was taken from the roundabout at St Andrew's Cross, which was built on the bomb-site at the top of Royal Parade. Old Town Street was also realigned at this time. Most of the buildings on the west side have been completed, but the old Drake's Circus block still stands in the distance (see page 76). Later it was demolished, and the present-day precinct was started in 1968. It was opened by HRH Princess Anne on 16 November 1971. Albert Pengelly's tobacconist shop on the corner presumably replaced his shop at the top of Union Street (see page 73).

New George Street, *c.* 1960. This was the old Frankfort Street and is now the bottom end of New George Street, running parallel with Royal Parade. Armada Way is running across the picture in the foreground. The *Western Morning News* office (Leicester Harmsworth House) is on the left, and from its angle to the new road you can see that Frankfort Street ran down to the right, towards the Odeon Cinema seen at the bottom. The Odeon originally opened as the Regent on 21 November 1931. It was one of the largest cinemas in Europe, seating 3,250. It was renamed the Odeon on 17 June 1940. It finally closed on 8 September 1962 and the old Gaumont in Union Street was renamed the Odeon two days later. A Littlewoods store was built on the old Odeon site. Woolworths is also at the bottom of this street on the right, and was one of the first shops to be opened in the city centre. The massive Prudential Building had stood, in alignment with the newspaper offices, on this left corner. Many people will have memories of open-air markets like 'Tin Pan Alley' in Radford Place and other sites like these in the picture, where a bit of initiative, and reasonable prices, provided a way of making a living.

Two views of modern Plymouth to complete this section. The top photograph shows the Royal Parade as seen from St Andrew's Cross. The tall Civic Centre building can be seen behind the Guildhall on the left. The lower photograph was taken from Smeaton's Tower on the Hoe, and shows the Naval War Memorial with Armada Way stretching away towards North Cross in the distance.

THE CATTEWATER &

SUTTON HARBOUR

The Cattewater and the Citadel, c. 1910.

Mount Batten, *c.* 1904. This is a view across the mouth of the Cattewater from Madeira Road and shows part of the Citadel in the foreground, with the Mount Batten peninsula and breakwater in the middle distance, and Staddon Heights in the background. The high cliff face is a prominent feature of Mount Batten and the tower on its top was built in the 1670s to help defend the Cattewater from attack from the sea. The place derives its name from a Captain Batten who defended Plymouth during the Royalist siege in the Civil War. Mount Batten was an RAF base and Aircraftsman Shaw, 'Lawrence of Arabia', served there in the 1930s. It was a seaplane base during the war, and, in recent times became an RAF Air/Sea Rescue Centre. The RAF Base was closed in July 1992 and the base is now in the care of the Plymouth Development Corporation.

Phoenix Wharf, *c.* 1905. The Oreston Steamboat Company started running a ferry service from Oreston and Turnchapel to the Barbican Pier on 3 May 1869. Then the service moved to Phoenix Wharf when it was built in 1895. The ferries were often packed with day trippers and the fare was one old penny each way.

Turnchapel Pier, with Mount Batten Tower in the distance, *c.* 1905. An evocative picture of three red-funnelled steamboats of the Oreston & Turnchapel Company at Turnchapel Pier with steam hanging in the sky. The boats are difficult to identify individually, but the company's boats have names like *Lively, Rapid, Dart* and *Swift*. In the 1880s there was stiff competition between Henry Elford's red-funnelled steamers and Greaney's yellow-funnelled steamers. Elford then built the Turnchapel Pier, at a cost of £1,000, and thus cornered the trade. Within two years Greaney had sold his boats to the Oreston & Turnchapel Company. The ferry service was extended to include Hooe, Cattedown and Mount Batten. There were also steamer trips from Phoenix Wharf to Bovisand beach and the golf links at Staddon Heights. However, with the growth of rail and road travel, the ferry business gradually declined and the service stopped in the mid-1960s.

Barbican Steps and entrance to Sutton Harbour, 1904. Viewed from Commercial Road, the West Pier is on the left and the East Pier and Coxside on the right. Sutton Harbour was vulnerable to storms before the Plymouth breakwater was built, and Captain (later Admiral) John MacBride, the local MP from 1784 to 1790, obtained government grants to build these two piers. The work was completed in 1800 and this greatly improved the harbour as a safe haven.

The Elizabethan House, New Street. It was built in 1580 during the prosperous Elizabethan years of Drake and Hawkins. Today this carefully restored merchants' house is open to the public and provides an interesting glimpse into the sixteenth century.

East and West Piers, *c.* 1915. A rather rustic view of the MacBride Piers shows Coxside, Teats Hill Road, and the gasometers on the far (east) side.

The Barbican from the West Pier, *c.* 1934. The Admiral MacBride Inn stands opposite the West Pier (to the left of the tall building), and commemorates his work towards the building of the piers. In the fourteenth century, Lambhay Castle stood on the hill to the left of this picture: the outer defences of a castle were called a 'barbican', so the whole of this ancient waterside thereby became known as the Barbican. A Mayflower Memorial was erected on the pier in 1934, to commemorate the sailing of the Mayflower with the Pilgrim Fathers in 1620.

The pleasure boat *Western Belle* in Sutton Harbour, *c.* 1930.

Barbican Fish Market, *c.* 1911. Fishermen are scrubbing sails laid out on the pier, with the fish market in the background and the spire of Charles Church in the distance.

Sutton Harbour and the fishing fleet, *c*. 1902. Southside Street and the Navy Hotel are on the left of the fish market, and North Quay is at the head of the harbour. In ancient times, Plympton, further up the Cattewater, was a prosperous port. It eventually became silted up and unworkable and Sutton Harbour became the major port: Plymouth grew from this area. The Barbican largely escaped the bombing of 1941 and is now the most ancient part of Plymouth and a conservation area. The harbour is now being developed; new lock gates have been installed and a new fish market opened in 1995.

The Cattewater and Laira from Turnchapel, *c.* 1904. The River Plym flows from Dartmoor to Plymouth Sound and the stretch from Laira Bridge to the Sound is called the Cattewater. In this view Cattedown is on the left with Oreston on the right. Laira Bridge can be seen in the distance. It is a cast-iron bridge, built by James Meadows Rendel, and was opened by the Duchess of Clarence (later Queen Adelaide) on 14 July 1827. The iron bridge then remained a toll bridge until 1924. In 1892 a railway bridge was opened beside the existing road bridge to carry the Plymouth & Dartmoor railway line to Plymstock. The Laira Bridge has now been demolished and replaced with a larger bridge that has a dual carriageway: this was opened on 1 June 1962.

Lee Moor Tramway, *c.* 1910. The tramway was used to transport china clay from Cann Quarry, on the River Plym near Plym Bridge, to the wharves at Laira. It was a familiar sight to see two horses pulling three or four open tramway wagons, or even three horses pulling seven wagons. The photographer shows the early delivery van with children at play as the horses go by.

SCHOOLDAYS
& SPORT

St James the Less Church, Citadel Road,

West Hoe, c. 1904.

Infant classes, St James the Less Church of England Primary School, West Hoe: top picture, 1904; lower picture, 1900. Two school photographs of lovely round faced children of long ago: four and five year olds, some clutching their precious toy animals; all looking charming and attentive, and a credit to their lady teachers. In the top picture, Edith Foote is in the middle of the second row from the front; in the lower picture her brother Fred is on the left end of the second row from the back, beside the teacher.

Infant class, St James the Less School, West Hoe, 1935. Another generation of five- and six-year-old children from the same school. Front row: fourth from the left, Arthur Sprague; fifth from the left, Brian Maloney. Second row: on the left, John Murch; fourth from the left, Beryl Elworthy; fifth from the left, Margo Rayner; sixth from the left, Barbara Cagett; seventh from the left, Marion Norman. Third row: extreme right, Muriel Harris. Back row: on the left, Gordon Davies; sixth from the left, Joan Bennett.

Infant Class, St James the Less School, West Hoe, 1937. Front row: on the left, Terry Malony; fifth from the left, Barbara Caggett; sixth from the left, Margo Rayner; seventh from the left, Beryl Elworthy; on the extreme right, Brian Malony. Second row: fourth from the left, June Fitzgerald; seventh from the left, Muriel Harris. Back row: second from the left, Freda Jackson; third from the left, Jill Venn; fourth from the left, June Burgoyne; fifth from the left, June Amerlaan; seventh from the left, Joan Bennett. St James the Less Church was destroyed during the Blitz on Plymouth in 1941, and was rebuilt after the war on the Ham Estate. St Andrew's Primary School was then built on the site in Citadel Road.

Ford Primary/Junior School, 1935–6. Front row of desks: second from right, Pamela Waldron (my wife). Second row: extreme right, Gordon Hawkins; second from right, June Pearce. Third row: fourth from right, Shirley Waldron. Fourth row: second from right, Georgina James. Fifth row: John Mills (with badge on jumper). Standing on the extreme left is Leonard Paramore. The girl fourth from the right is one of twins with her sister also dressed in a pinafore in the second row. The children sit at their desks with chalks, slates and dusters for written work. The boy standing on the right at the back has his overcoat on and his 'FJS' cap clasped to his chest, ready for a quick getaway.

Junior class, Ford Primary/Junior School, 1936–7. Front row: fifth from the left, Pamela Waldron; on the extreme right, Phyllis Rowlands. Second row: fourth from the left, Georgina James; sixth from the left, Shirley Waldron; second from the right, Margaret White. Third row: sixth from the left, John Mills. Back row: second from the left, Gordon Hawkins.

Torpoint Athletic III Team, winners of the Plymouth Combination Junior Cup, 1947–8. Back row, left to right: Frank Searle, Jack Kingston (committee members), Bill Snell, Jim Osborne, Ray Williams, Brian Nickels, Tom Bowden, Ted Short (chairman). Middle row: Johnny Richards, John Conyon, Brian Cardew (captain), Geoff Peach, David Paul. Front row: Derrick Warmington, Peter Waye. We had a good team in those days, with a few 'stars' and a solid defence. I couldn't get into the team so I appear in the picture as a reserve. I suppose we all experience disappointments in life, and we should keep a stiff upper lip and try harder! I went off and played rugby instead.

Plymouth Argyle Football Team, 1931–2. Back row, left to right: R. Bowden, P. Thompson, F. Cosgrove, H. Bland, H. Cann, G. Hanbury, F. Titmus, W. Price, F. Harris. Middle row: S. Attenbury (trainer), D. Mackay, N. Mackay, W. Fellowes, F. McKenzie, J. Pullen, A. Hardie, T. Haynes (trainer). Front row: A. Matthews, J. Healey, T. Grozier, F. Sloan, J. Vidler, J. Leslie, S. Black, D. Prentice, J. Lietch. Argyle won promotion in the 1930–1 season. Here they are seen with the Third Division South Championship Trophy (right), and the Southern League Championship Trophy.

St Columba Rugby Team, 1954–5. Back row, left to right: P.G. Clements, W.L. Copley, E.J.C. Summers (secretary), R.F. Bunney, T.V. Yabsley. Middle row: R.H. Graver (vice-president), P.C. Summers, R.W. Widdicombe, Tom Bowden, F.P.E. Goodman, D.J. Rowe, D.A. Rendle, B.A. Curnow, W.H. Drayton, H.J. Lear (trainer). Front row: J. Horsham (treasurer), M. Summers, M.C.T. Reilly FRCS (chairman), E. Dean (captain), N. Campbell (president), H. Rowe, F. Rowe (vice-chairman). The club had a home ground at Elburton when I played, and later they moved to Torpoint. We had a number of good players, of whom Len Copley, of Devonport Services, the Navy, and England trialist, was probably the best.

Torpoint Bowls Team, winners of the Plymouth and District Bowling League, Division 2, in 1969. Front row, left to right: Bert Beaver, Daniel B. Peacock, Bill Jarvis, Ed Bawden, Frank Elliot, Jack Allen. Middle row: Tom Haddy, Charlie Greeno, Stan Jones, Bill Oliver, Phil Pugsley, James Bowden (my father), Ed Wilcox. Back row (in blazers): Ron Lowe, Charlie Hooper, Arthur Baker, Norman Mashford, Wilfred Honey, Albert Henley, Sidney Harris. The club was formed in 1923 and their bowling green is at Thanckes Park, on the site of the old Thanckes House.

Devonport Albion Rugby Football Club, 1908–9. Back row, left to right: W. George (committee), F.J. Lillicrap, C. Marshall, E. Carter (honorary secretary), W. Spiers, T. Hayman, J. Maker. Third row: W.E. Sowden (committee), R. Gilbert, S. Harris, G.H. Williams, A. Williams, D.R. Gordon, A.E. Day (trainer). Second row: S. Harvey, E.J. Vivyan, W.A. Mills (captain), F. Dean (vice-captain), T.H. Hawkings, H. Pope. Front row: R. Jago, J. Summers. Devonport Albion was formed in 1876 by dockyard apprentices and they moved to the Rectory ground in 1896. They were very successful in the period up to the First World War, but Devonport Services took over the Rectory ground in 1912 and the Devonport Albion club was then in difficulties, without a home ground. The Plymouth Rugby Club and the Devonport Albion Club amalgamated in about 1918 to become Plymouth Albion. Club premises were found at Beacon Park in 1919, and the 1920s were a golden era for the club, when five Albion players represented England in one international side.

Victoria Park, with a bandstand and sheep gently grazing, c. 1910. It had a number of football pitches in the 1940s when I played, and it seems much the same now. In the nineteenth century it was part of Mill Lake, which extended from Stonehouse Pool to Pennycomequick. Around the turn of the century the area above Millbridge was filled in to form Victoria Park. Some people will remember the Millbridge, with its half-penny toll, which continued until 1925.

Hoe Grammar School, *c.* 1920. The school opened in 1867 at 6 Lockyer Street and George Pearse Dymond became headmaster in 1887. Gradually the school was extended to 7 and 8 Lockyer Street, to 2 Alfred Street, and 11 Windsor Terrace. By the 1920s and '30s the school was very full and successful, with a wide range of academic and sports activities. Mr Dymond remained headmaster for over fifty years. In March 1941 Lockyer Street was straddled with high explosive and incendiary bombs and the orphanage next door, the YWCA and adjoining houses were burnt out. On 21 April 1941 the school premises were totally destroyed and the school was finished.

A youth string orchestra, *c.* 1910. Not much is known about this picture except that one of the boy mandolin players lived in Morice Town, Devonport. So could this be a gathering of young players at a school of music in Morice Town?

Section Eight

AROUND & ABOUT

Mouth of the River Yealm, c. 1910.

Bovisand Beach, Plymouth Sound, 1949. This is a popular bathing place. Bovisand Fort, on the skyline, is one of twenty-two such forts built around Plymouth by Lord Palmerston in the nineteenth century, to defend it against invasion from Napoleonic France. They were never required.

Mount Batten beach, south of Mount Batten breakwater, 1905. There's not a lot of sand, and the people sit or stroll around fully clothed. It's an interesting insight into Edwardian life. Note the business premises behind and Stamford Fort, the scene of fighting during the Civil War, in the background.

Hooe Lake, *c.* 1920. A view from above Hooelake Quarry with the old swing bridge on the left carrying the railway line from Turnchapel to Laira rail bridge and the Western Railway main line. Looking across Hooe Lake, Radford Quarry is on the left, Radford Lake in the middle, with the Castle (a folly) perched on Radford Weir. To the right is the quay at Hexton with houseboats lining the bank. Behind the freshwater Radford Lake is Burrow Hill, a local vantage point, with Radford Park Road running across the hillside. Today the railway line and swing bridge have gone. There are still many green spaces provided by Radford Park beyond Radford Lake, and the woods at Lower Hooe and Hexton. Hooe Lake is more silted up now and there are certainly more houses on the hills around.

Fore Street, Plympton, *c.* 1902, before the town became a part of Plymouth. This is the old A38 route straight through Plympton, a familiar scene to any mature motorist.

Dartmeet, on Dartmoor, *c.* 1905. Here the East and West Dart rivers join to flow down to Dartmouth. The road ahead wends its way to Two Bridges; the East Dart flows down from the right, with the West Dart seen coming down the middle of the picture. The Dart River disappears out of view to the left. It was a difficult place to get to in those days, but a favourite spot now for a picnic, or a cream tea at Badgers Holt tea rooms, with the children playing on the clapper bridge and by the river.

Badger's Holt, Dartmeet, *c.* 1920. Cream teas are being served in the garden, with the trees all around. The stately waitress is coming with a pot of tea, scones, strawberry jam, and a mountain of clotted cream, while the customers sit patiently, or munch away, and enjoy the lovely scenery.

Burrator Reservoir, Dartmoor, *c.* 1926. The reservoir was constructed between 1893 and 1898. The three towns amalgamated in 1914 and the joint water authority decided to increase water storage at the reservoir by adding an additional 10 ft to the height of the dam. This took 4½ years and the work was completed in 1928. The capacity was thereby increased from 650 million to over 1,000 million gallons, and this view shows the work in progress. A temporary suspension bridge has been erected to take the traffic whilst construction work is taking place on the dam.

Princetown Prison gate, Dartmoor, 1904. It looks much the same today. The convicts look like a chain gang just departing for a hard day's work, and are an interesting subject for an Edwardian postcard! Can you imagine sending one to a friend or relative, and saying, 'Having a lovely time in Plymouth and went to see the convicts yesterday'? Perhaps it was part of an anti-crime campaign, or a way of showing the harsh treatment of prisoners in these times.

Saltash Bridge and ferries, on the Plymouth side of the River Tamar, *c.* 1924. The famous Royal Albert Bridge at Saltash was designed and built by Isambard Kingdom Brunel. It was completed in May 1859 and is considered one of his greatest railway achievements. The river is 1,100 ft wide at this point and 70 ft deep at high tide. Also the admiralty required headroom of 100 ft to allow warships to pass safely underneath. Brunel's bridge spectacularly surmounted all problems. The ancient town of Saltash had its first ferry in the fourteenth century; later this type of chain ferry was used. Here early motor cars are embarking on a steam-driven ferry, while the standby ferry is moored at the water's edge. When the new road bridge was completed in 1961, the ferry was taken out of service, to the annoyance of many local people.

Royal Albert Bridge, from Saltash, *c.* 1905. The site chosen demanded curved approaches and therefore precluded a suspension bridge design, which requires supporting chains anchored at each end. Brunel decided to use these two large central beams, each 465 ft long, to take the load and thus required only one central support in mid-stream with deep-water foundations. Note the single-track line and how the sides of the bridge are composed of straight wrought-iron sections. Saltash Pier is in the foreground.

Saltash foreshore, *c*. 1905. An example of the patient art of the professional photographer. The little boy, wearing a tie, sits on a bollard, and all the giggling girls and boys crowd around. We have the rugged foreshore, the bridge and pier, training ship *Mount Edgcumbe* and Ernesettle in the background – but the photographer is still waiting for a train to come along! The *Mount Edgcumbe* was moored off Saltash and used for training homeless and destitute boys for the navy. There were about 250 boys on board, aged between twelve and sixteen, and discipline was hard. The training establishment was closed in December 1920 and the ship broken up.

The Hamoaze and Bull Point, *c*. 1910. A view across the river from Saltash, showing Bull Point and the Hamoaze, with some warships in the foreground, and Wilcove and Torpoint in the distance.

HMS *Defiance*, moored in the River Lynher off Wearde Quay, near Saltash, *c.* 1905. *Defiance* was the Royal Navy's torpedo school. The ships forming the school changed, but here seem to comprise *Defiance* on the right, with *Perseus* in the middle (with a tender alongside), and *Flamingo* on the left. HMS *Defiance* was built at Pembroke in 1861, a wooden ship of 5,270 tons, but with the advent of ironclad ships she was already obsolete. She was commissioned at Wearde Quay in 1884, and the GWR established *Defiance* Halt for their use. In October 1930 the establishment moved to a berth off Wilcove, and in 1931 the original *Defiance*, then seventy years old, was withdrawn, then sold and broken up in Millbay Docks. The school was finally closed in 1959.

Torpoint Ferry, *c.* 1908. Two old-style ferries of differing designs, one in use and the other moored off-shore. There has been a ferry at Torpoint since about 1730, but it was not until 1834 that J.M. Rendel built the first ferry with a steam reciprocating engine to pull the ferry across the river on chains and beat the tides. Now there are three diesel-driven ferries, among the biggest river ferries in the world, but we still get long queues at times!

SS *Lady Beatrice*, *c*. 1910. She was a small coal-burning, propeller-driven steamer, plying from Torpoint across to North Corner and Pottery Quay, on the Devonport side. The round trip took about forty-five minutes and cost 1d. You can see it was very popular! The steamer was named after the first wife of Sir John Pole-Carew, of Antony House, outside Torpoint. In the background are the chimneys of the Dockyard power station and the spire of St James's Church in Keyham Road (which once housed the Dockyard School); both have long since disappeared.

Emma and William Martin Devereux, my maternal grandparents, *c*. 1915. Martin Devereux was the captain of the ferry boat, *Lady Beatrice*. I remember him as an old man with drooping moustache and ulcerated legs, listening to his 'cats-whisker' radio. My grandmother was Emma Maria Woodrow Pengelly of Looe before she married. She died in 1926 before I was born. Sadly, the photograph is damaged and Martin has become obscured, but Emma still shines out off the page.

Antony Road, leading out of Torpoint, *c.* 1910. On the left is the Ellis Memorial. This was erected in memory of James Benjamin Ellis who lost his life in July 1897 saving two boys from drowning when they got into difficulties while bathing near Torpoint Ballast Pond. Today, the memorial is still here, but re-positioned in Sparrow Park. Motorists will remember this road as the place where they queued for the ferry!

Tamar Street, Torpoint, *c.* 1904. This is the street leading from Fore Street to the Torpoint Ferry. On the left is The Institute with reading room and assembly hall. Further along that side is the Bible Christian Chapel, now the Conservative Club, and at the end of the street is the old police station. The block on the right was named East Cornwall House and there were council offices above the shops until 1936–7. The shops could have been Down's, Kent's, or Tozer's shops at this time. Around the far right-hand corner is the Queen's Arms, which is still in business. In the centre of the picture is a water cart for damping the dusty road. The Institute and East Cornwall House were bombed during the war and the area was then re-developed.

The 'Comrades', Torpoint, *c*. 1936. In the foreground is Antony Road, about half-way up the hill out of Torpoint. Moor View Road is on the left. Intriguingly, the photographer has chosen this view from the middle of the allotments, and among the overhead cables! The wooden hut beside the road is the Torpoint & District Comrades and United Services Club. On the left is Albion Road School, which I attended years ago, and further away can be seen the oil storage tanks in Thanckes Depot, and Saltash Bridge with those massive curved beams. On the right is the Hamoaze and the dockyard, with ships moored 'up the trot'. Today, the 'Comrades' have a modern clubhouse built on the old allotments. New schools have been built in Trevol Road and my old school is now Albion Road Infants and Nursery School. I remember the school playgrounds and my playmates who were killed in the air-raids. During the heavy bombing of 1941 we got a lift on a coal lorry every night to sleep in a church hall in the relative safety of Polbathic. I was only eleven but I can still hear the women sobbing in the night.

Mum and me in 1933. This photograph was taken in Jerome Studios, Plymouth, on my fourth birthday. I didn't seem too pleased about having to stand still and look at the photographer. My mother was named Emma Woodrow, after her mother, and she was born in Surrey Cottage, Woolster Street, the Barbican, Plymouth, on 22 May 1905. At that time her father was the captain of a tugboat based in Sutton Harbour.

Torpoint Ballast Pond, 1977. This was built for the Navy in 1783 to house lighters (barges) which were used for ballasting men-o'-war. It looks as it did when I was a child and lived in Navy Terrace, opposite the pond. We kids searched for shrapnel and incendiary bombs in the mud and I found a ton of the stuff! My special treasure was a beautiful, finless, silver bomb which I found on the Ballast Pond. I unscrewed the detonator cap, knocked out the 'powder', and took it home for my collection under the bed. There was a carbine rifle and a 0.22 rifle which American soldiers camped in Fore Street, Devonport, had given me, a bayonet, a hand grenade, and now this incendiary bomb! I think Dad gave it all away under an amnesty. In the background, left to right, is the supply ship *Fort Grange* at a jetty in South Yard, then Cremyll, Mashford's Yard, and Maker Heights. The Ballast Pond has now been transformed into a popular marina.

Thanckes House, Torpoint, *c*. 1904. The Graves family lived on this estate in the mid-eighteenth century. Admiral Thomas Graves led the Van Division at the great sea battle of 1794 against the French off Ushant, known as the 'Glorious First of June', and was afterwards created Baron Graves. This mansion was built in 1871. Around 1900, Thanckes House passed from the Graves family to Sir Reginald Pole-Carew. In 1909 the house was dismantled stone by stone and re-erected 6 miles away at Portwrinkle, with the tower at the other end. The Tudor Gothic building, of Cornish dressed limestone, was opened in July 1910 as the Whitsand Bay Hotel. Torpoint Bowling Green now stands on the original foundations, beside the walled garden, the tennis courts, and overlooking the Hamoaze.

Torpoint Lawn, below Thanckes tennis courts, 1922. This was part of Thanckes estate and General Sir Reginald Pole-Carew presented the estate to the town in 1925. The Lawn had a tea-hut and a swimming pool, and families came from Plymouth and Devonport to enjoy a day out. The pool was closed after the war and the area turfed over. Today the Lawn is part of Thanckes Park.

Southdown, Millbrook Lake, and the Hamoaze, viewed from Maker, *c.* 1940. Southdown, with its chimneys, is in the foreground, and Foss is just out of view on the left. In the nineteenth century there had been many industries in Southdown and Foss. There were brickworks, quarries, a gunpowder mill, soap factory, copper smelter, brewery, fish fertilizer works, and glue factory at various times. They declined over the years for various reasons and now they have all gone. Devonport is across the river, and Dartmoor can be seen in the distance.

Millbrook Lake, viewed from Maker, *c.* 1904. Anderton is in the foreground and Millbrook in the distance. Note the old tide mill and millpond, with All Saints' Church nearby. Today the millpond has been filled in and the land reclaimed as a recreation area. Also, the upper reaches of the lake have been dammed as part of a flood prevention scheme.

Two views of Cremyll Point, 1904. This is the narrowest part of the harbour, where there is a ferry service to Admiral's Hard on the Plymouth side. In ancient times the ferry formed part of a route into Cornwall. It became very busy when the Naval Dockyard was being built in the eighteenth century, but it wasn't until 1885 that the old rowing boats were replaced by a steamboat named *Dodo*. The Tower House and quay can be seen above, with Devil's Point in the distance. Below is the ferry landing place, with a horse-drawn carriage to take passengers to Millbrook. The naval training ship *Impregnable* and other training hulks are moored off shore. The Edgcumbe Arms stands on the quay; the pub got very busy with passing trade, and with many naval customers carousing at weekends! The Tower House was demolished by a bomb in 1941, and the training ships have long disappeared to a breaker's yard. The Edgcumbe Arms was gutted in a fire recently, so we'll have to wait for that drink, but the ferry service is still going strong.

HMS *Impregnable*, the Hamoaze and Dockyard from Cremyll, *c.* 1903. HMS *Impregnable* was originally named HMS *Howe* when she was launched in 1860; she was one of the last wooden battleships. She never went to sea in anger and was laid up in the Hamoaze for twenty-five years before being brought into service as a training ship for boy sailors in 1885, and renamed HMS *Impregnable*. Note the old covered slipways in the Dockyard, and the Hamoaze extending up-river to Saltash.

HMS *Nile* in the Hamoaze, *c.* 1902. She was port guard ship from 1893 to 1903, and remained at Devonport until sold and broken up in 1912. HMS *Nile* was sister ship to HMS *Trafalgar*, with a displacement of over 12,000, tons and was fitted with 13½ in guns. The covered slipways are seen again in the background, with Mutton Cove on the right, and the King Billy statue in between.

Mount Edgcumbe House, 1903. Piers, son of the legendary Sir Richard Edgcumbe, married Joan Durnford, heiress to the Stonehouse lands, thus inheriting land on both sides of the Tamar, including Mount Edgcumbe Park. His son, Sir Richard Edgcumbe, built Mount Edgcumbe House in 1553 and the family moved from Cotehele. On 22 April 1941, during the Blitz on Plymouth, Mount Edgcumbe House was gutted by stray incendiary bombs. Kenelm Edgcumbe (1873–1965), the 6th Earl, rebuilt the house, and it was completed in 1958. Today the house and country park, covering 864 acres, are owned jointly by Plymouth City Council and Cornwall County Council. It is open to the general public and thousands of people enjoy this beautiful place each year.

'The Folly', Mount Edgcumbe Park, *c.* 1900. It was built by Richard, 1st Baron of Mount Edgcumbe, in 1747 as a picturesque ruin. Richard had been MP for Plympton for forty years. He was fond of his dog, and when the animal died he put its skeleton in the garden house so that he could be near his old friend! Here is one last look across Plymouth Sound with Drake's Island, the Hoe, the Cattewater, and then Dartmoor in the distance.

Cawsand, Cawsand Bay, *c.* 1920. The village looks peaceful here, with a pleasure boat arrived from Plymouth Pier, but in the nineteenth century it was an exciting place with trading and fishing, and a little smuggling.

Acknowledgements

This is my opportunity to thank all those who have assisted me with the loan of photographs, or permission to use photographs, for the supply of information, or just wise counsel and the sharing of knowledge. It is very rewarding when your friends, acquaintances, and other generous people come to your aid. I am extremely grateful to all the following:

Mr and Mrs R. Ball • Mr A.L. Clamp • Mrs M. Farran • Mrs E. Johns
Mr R. Lowe • Mr R.J. Mahony • Mr and Mrs P. Manning
Mr and Mrs C. Prout • Mrs D. Ratcliffe • Mr S. Rendell
The churchwardens of St Andrew's Church, Plymouth.

BRITAIN IN OLD PHOTOGRAPHS

To order any of these titles please telephone Littlehampton Book Services on 01903 721596

Scunthorpe, *D Taylor*
Skegness, *W Kime*
Around Skegness, *W Kime*

LONDON

Balham and Tooting, *P Loobey*
Crystal Palace, Penge & Anerley, *M Scott*
Greenwich and Woolwich, *K Clark*
Hackney: A Second Selection, *D Mander*
Lewisham and Deptford, *J Coulter*
Lewisham and Deptford: A Second Selection, *J Coulter*
Streatham, *P Loobey*
Around Whetstone and North Finchley, *J Heathfield*
Woolwich, *B Evans*

MONMOUTHSHIRE

Chepstow and the River Wye, *A Rainsbury*
Monmouth and the River Wye, *Monmouth Museum*

NORFOLK

Great Yarmouth, *M Teun*
Norwich, *M Colman*
Wymondham and Attleborough, *P Yaxley*

NORTHAMPTONSHIRE

Around Stony Stratford, *A Lambert*

NOTTINGHAMSHIRE

Arnold and Bestwood, *M Spick*
Arnold and Bestwood: A Second Selection, *M Spick*
Changing Face of Nottingham, *G Oldfield*
Mansfield, *Old Mansfield Society*
Around Newark, *T Warner*
Nottingham: 1944–1974, *D Whitworth*
Sherwood Forest, *D Ottewell*
Victorian Nottingham, *M Payne*

OXFORDSHIRE

Around Abingdon, *P Horn*
Banburyshire, *M Barnett & S Gosling*
Burford, *A Jewell*
Around Didcot and the Hagbournes, *B Lingham*
Garsington, *M Gunther*
Around Henley-on-Thames, *S Ellis*
Oxford: The University, *J Rhodes*
Thame to Watlington, *N Hood*
Around Wallingford, *D Beasley*
Witney, *T Worley*
Around Witney, *C Mitchell*
Witney District, *T Worley*
Around Woodstock, *J Bond*

POWYS

Brecon, *Brecknock Museum*
Welshpool, *E Bredsdorff*

SHROPSHIRE

Shrewsbury, *D Trumper*
Whitchurch to Market Drayton, *M Morris*

SOMERSET

Bath, *J Hudson*
Bridgwater and the River Parrett, *R Fitzhugh*
Bristol, *D Moorcroft & N Campbell-Sharp*
Changing Face of Keynsham,
  B Lowe & M Whitehead

Chard and Ilminster, *G Gosling & F Huddy*
Crewkerne and the Ham Stone Villages,
  G Gosling & F Huddy
Around Keynsham and Saltford, *B Lowe & T Brown*
Midsomer Norton and Radstock, *C Howell*
Somerton, Ilchester and Langport, *G Gosling & F Huddy*
Taunton, *N Chipchase*
Around Taunton, *N Chipchase*
Wells, *C Howell*
Weston-Super-Mare, *S Poole*
Around Weston-Super-Mare, *S Poole*
West Somerset Villages, *K Houghton & L Thomas*

STAFFORDSHIRE

Aldridge, *J Farrow*
Bilston, *E Rees*
Black Country Transport: Aviation, *A Brew*
Around Burton upon Trent, *G Sowerby & R Farman*
Bushbury, *A Chatwin, M Mills & E Rees*
Around Cannock, *M Mills & S Belcher*
Around Leek, *R Poole*
Lichfield, *H Clayton & K Simmons*
Around Pattingham and Wombourne, *M Griffiths,*
  P Leigh & M Mills
Around Rugeley, *T Randall & J Anslow*
Smethwick, *J Maddison*
Stafford, *J Anslow & T Randall*
Around Stafford, *J Anslow & T Randall*
Stoke-on-Trent, *J Anslow & T Randall*
Around Tamworth, *R Sulima*
Around Tettenhall and Codsall, *M Mills*
Tipton, Wednesbury and Darlaston, *R Pearson*
Walsall, *D Gilbert & M Lewis*
Wednesbury, *I Bott*
West Bromwich, *R Pearson*

SUFFOLK

Ipswich: A Second Selection, *D Kindred*
Around Ipswich, *D Kindred*
Around Mildenhall, *C Dring*
Southwold to Aldeburgh, *H Phelps*
Around Woodbridge, *H Phelps*

SURREY

Cheam and Belmont, *P Berry*
Croydon, *S Bligh*
Dorking and District, *K Harding*
Around Dorking, *A Jackson*
Around Epsom, *P Berry*
Farnham: A Second Selection, *J Parratt*
Around Haslemere and Hindhead, *T Winter & G Collyer*
Richmond, *Richmond Local History Society*
Sutton, *P Berry*

SUSSEX

Arundel and the Arun Valley, *J Godfrey*
Bishopstone and Seaford, *P Pople & P Berry*
Brighton and Hove, *J Middleton*
Brighton and Hove: A Second Selection, *J Middleton*
Around Crawley, *M Goldsmith*
Hastings, *P Haines*
Hastings: A Second Selection, *P Haines*
Around Haywards Heath, *J Middleton*
Around Heathfield, *A Gillet & B Russell*
Around Heathfield: A Second Selection,
  A Gillet & B Russell
High Weald, *B Harwood*
High Weald: A Second Selection, *B Harwood*
Horsham and District, *T Wales*

Lewes, *J Middleton*
RAF Tangmere, *A Saunders*
Around Rye, *A Dickinson*
Around Worthing, *S White*

WARWICKSHIRE

Along the Avon from Stratford to Tewkesbury, *J Jeremiah*
Bedworth, *J Burton*
Coventry, *D McGrory*
Around Coventry, *D McGrory*
Nuneaton, *S Clews & S Vaughan*
Around Royal Leamington Spa, *J Cameron*
Around Royal Leamington Spa: A Second Selection,
  J Cameron
Around Warwick, *R Booth*

WESTMORLAND

Eden Valley, *J Marsh*
Kendal, *M & P Duff*
South Westmorland Villages, *J Marsh*
Westmorland Lakes, *J Marsh*

WILTSHIRE

Around Amesbury, *P Daniels*
Chippenham and Lacock, *A Wilson & M Wilson*
Around Corsham and Box, *A Wilson & M Wilson*
Around Devizes, *D Buxton*
Around Highworth, *G Tanner*
Around Highworth and Faringdon, *G Tanner*
Around Malmesbury, *A Wilson*
Marlborough: A Second Selection, *P Colman*
Around Melksham,
  Melksham and District Historical Association
Nadder Valley, *R. Sawyer*
Salisbury, *P Saunders*
Salisbury: A Second Selection, *P Daniels*
Salisbury: A Third Selection, *P Daniels*
Around Salisbury, *P Daniels*
Swindon: A Third Selection, *The Swindon Society*
Swindon: A Fourth Selection, *The Swindon Society*
Trowbridge, *M Marshman*
Around Wilton, *P Daniels*
Around Wootton Bassett, Cricklade and Purton, *T Sharp*

WORCESTERSHIRE

Evesham to Bredon, *F Archer*
Around Malvern, *K Smith*
Around Pershore, *M Dowty*
Redditch and the Needle District, *R Saunders*
Redditch: A Second Selection, *R Saunders*
Around Tenbury Wells, *D Green*
Worcester, *M Dowty*
Around Worcester, *R Jones*
Worcester in a Day, *M Dowty*
Worcestershire at Work, *R Jones*

YORKSHIRE

Huddersfield: A Second Selection, *H Wheeler*
Huddersfield: A Third Selection, *H Wheeler*
Leeds Road and Rail, *R Vickers*
Pontefract, *R van Riel*
Scarborough, *D Coggins*
Scarborough's War Years, *R Percy*
Skipton and the Dales, *Friends of the Craven Museum*
Around Skipton-in-Craven, *Friends of the Craven Museum*
Yorkshire Wolds, *I & M Sumner*